A B C
HAWAII

*Dedicated to my parents,
Wilfred and Miriam Mita,
and to my wife, Marion.*

With special thanks to Wayne Kimura and
Robert Schmitt for their assistance in
gathering the data for this book and to the
State of Hawaii's Department of Business
Economic Development and Tourism for
use of information in their publication *The
State of Hawaii Data Book, 1992.*

Mutual Publishing
1127 11th Ave., Mezzanine B
Honolulu, Hawaii 96816
Tel (808) 732-1709
FAX (808) 734-4094

Printed in Korea

ABC Hawaii is the first in a
series of titles for today's highly
curious traveler that carries the
imprint of *This Week Publications* on
the cover. Travelogues for each
island and Waikiki will soon follow.
These books will focus on the multi-
experiences and diversity offered by
the Hawaiian Islands.

For nearly three decades, *This
Week* Magazines have informed
millions of Hawaii's visitors about
the Aloha State. During the last few
years our readers began requesting
more detailed and specific information about what to see and do when
in Hawaii. They were no longer
coming to the islands only for the
beach or for the scenery, but were
after a vacation experience ranging
from light to highly active recreational activities. They were
interested in golfing, tennis, fishing,
sailing, snorkeling, scuba diving,
hiking, bicycling, participating in an
athletic tournament, getting or staying
physically fit, and observing or
participating in cultural or ecological
tourism.

To provide all the answers in our
publications would go beyond our
magazine's intent to be a source of
current information and tourist news.
Instead *This Week* Magazines have
arranged with Mutual Publishing for
a number of titles providing in-depth
descriptions about the Islands aimed
at today's energetic, sophisticated
traveler.

ABC HAWAII

AN ILLUSTRATED REFERENCE GUIDE

EVERYTHING TO KNOW
ABOUT THE ISLANDS

Compilation:
Randall T. Mita, M.D.

Major Photography:
Douglas Peebles

Design:
Gonzalez Design Company

Mutual Publishing

The charm of Waikiki

TABLE OF CONTENTS

TRAVEL HINTS

BEFORE YOU GET HERE

• **Camera**. Make sure you bring one. If you get a new camera for the trip, familiarize yourself with it. Shoot a test roll or two. Hawaii has a lot to photograph and you will want all the pictures to come out.

• **Climate**. Come prepared for warm weather. Bring a swimsuit, a hat, a long-sleeve shirt, and sun screen. See "Weather" under General Information.

• **Planning**. Your own travel agent is the best source of information. But you may want to phone or write the Hawaii Visitors Bureau, 2270 Kalakaua Ave., Suite 801, Honolulu, HI 96815. Tel. (808) 923-1811; Fax (808) 922-8991; Telex 8483 HVB HR). Request a copy of *He Kukini*, which has information on coming events as well as facts and hints to help you enjoy your vacation. The friendly HVB staff can furnish answers to special questions.

• **Previewing**. Do a pre-tour of Hawaii with a book such as this. Then, before you board your plane, either have your travel agent book the appropriate tours or arrange enough free time to handle it yourself. Early reservations make it possible to do the things you want, when you want them.

AFTER YOU ARRIVE HERE

• **Currency**. Standard U.S. dollars, major credit cards, traveler's checks. Some foreign currencies accepted also.

• **Driving**. **1) When you park your car at a scenic location, always lock it and take your valuables with you.** 2) For safety's sake, buckle your seat belt while driving. If you need more incentive, there is a $50 fine if you are caught not wearing one. 3) No open alcohol containers are allowed in cars either moving or parked on a city street.

• **What to do books**. Available free at airports, in hotel lobbies, on the street in visitor areas such as Waikiki and Lahaina, and at Hawaii Visitors Bureau offices. They contain valuable discount coupons, travel hints, maps, and informative articles.

• **Tipping**. Unless otherwise specified, tipping is appreciated by your hosts. Generally, $1 per person is right for day tours, and 10 to 15 percent at restaurants.

• **Sun**. *Be careful*. In Hawaii it will fry you, even on cloudy days. If you want some sun, start early in the morning with 15 minutes or less daily. You can tolerate more time if you use a sunscreen with sun protective factor (SPF) 8 to 15. Using a sunscreen is *always* a good idea; sunburn in Paradise is no fun. Sunglasses and a broad-brim hat also help.

INTRODUCTION

Hawaii achieved U.S. Statehood in 1959 but, for many visitors, the islands remain less a State than a state of mind.

That state of mind leads them to expect "paradise," a cheerful fantasy nurtured for decades by Hawaii's visitor industry. The fantasy has worked well. State planners expect 10 million visitors annually by the year 2000.

Many will be seeking "paradise," a palm-fringed Never-Never Land where playful mermaids serve blue cocktails, where no one grows old, where it rains only at night. Actually, Hawaii is not a total paradise. It is far more interesting. It is a real place.

If you are willing to forego the mermaids and blue cocktails, this book will help you discover the real Hawaii. You will find a land of weather and waves and winter whales, where a polyglot people have shared an extraordinary history and together have forged a diverse, dynamic society, like no other.

Equal parts American, Asian and Polynesian, Hawaii today finds itself on the leading edge of what social thinkers have termed "the Pacific century." Those who come here with their hearts, minds and senses open—those who seek the real Hawaii rather than the fantasy—will become part of this Pacific adventure.

To that end, *ABC Hawaii—An Illustrated Reference Guide* not only explores scenic attractions and recreational offerings, but speaks as well of Hawaii's Polynesian and Asian heritage—from "aloha" to "zori."

Clearly, simply written and alphabetized for speedy reference, *ABC Hawaii* is both thorough and concise—a user-friendly companion on a journey to a real place.

Start with the General Information section. It covers the spectrum of Hawaii, from the many meanings of "aloha" to current styles in island footwear, and from tennis etiquette to the geology of volcanoes.

Each of Hawaii's islands has its own distinctive character. The Island chapters offer essential facts, followed by practical tour suggestions. Extended alphabetical listings of important scenic, cultural, and historical sites complete each island-chapter. Read and remember, and you will feel at home among Hawaii's people, flora and history.

A glossary of frequently heard Hawaiian words, a brief survey of highlights of the Islands' last thousand years, a special section on flora, some suggestions for further reading, and a wealth of carefully selected photographs make this an unusually useful guide to your Hawaiian odyssey.

Phone numbers, hours of operation, and prices are subject to change. For current information on places to go and see, inquire at your hotel's concierge desk or telephone directory. Numbers are listed in the yellow pages telephone directory.

E Komo Mai! Welcome to Hawaii, where the rain may fall but the sun always shines.

The splendour of Kauai—Na Pali Coast

ANTHEM

Hawaii has a State anthem, "Hawaii Ponoi," written in 1874 by King David Kalakaua (1836-1891) as a tribute to Kamehameha the Great. German-born Heinrich Berger, at that time the leader of the Royal Hawaiian Band, composed the music. It is heard at most official functions.

Hawaii Ponoi	Hawaii's Own*
Hawaii ponoi,	*Hawaii's own,*
Nana i kou moi,	*Look to your king,*
Ka lani alii,	*The royal chief,*
Ke alii.	*The chief.*
Makua lani e,	*Royal father,*
Kamehameha e,	*Kamehameha,*
Na kaua e pale	*We shall defend*
Me ka ihe.	*With spears.*
Hawaii ponoi,	*Hawaii's own,*
Nana i na alii,	*Look to your chiefs,*
Na pua muli kou,	*The children after*
Na pokii.	*you, The young.*
Hawaii ponoi,	*Hawaii's own,*
E ka lahui e,	*O nation,*
O kau hana nui	*Your great duty*
E ui e.	*Strive.*

* Translation from Samuel H. Elbert and Mary Kawena Pukui, *Na Mele o Hawai'i Ne'i: 101 Hawaiian Songs*. Honolulu: University of Hawaii Press, 1970.

STATE BIRD

Nene (Branta sandwicensis)

The *nene*, or Hawaiian goose, is unique to these islands. Although still on the endangered list, the species is making a comeback, thanks to "managed" breeding programs. The webs of the *nene's* feet have shrunk to about half their original size in adaptation to the relatively waterless slopes of Haleakala on Maui and the mountains of the Big Island where they are found today.

STATE CAPITAL

State Capitol building, dedicated in 1969

Honolulu, on Oahu, the third largest of the Hawaiian Islands, became the capital in 1845 when Kamehameha III (the last son of Kamehameha the Great to rule) moved his government from Lahaina, Maui.

STATE FISH

Reef Triggerfish (Rhinecanthus rectangulu)

Most residents regard the *humuhumu-nukunukuapuaa* (pronounced hoo-moo hoo-moo noo-koo noo-koo ah poo-ah-ah), a triggerfish, as the State fish, although its "term of office" expired in 1990 and a successor had not yet been chosen. When threatened, this relatively slow-moving fish dives for a hole in the reef and locks itself in place with its "trigger" dorsal spine. Wedged in, it is usually safe from predators. In Hawaiian, *humu humu* means "to fit pieces together," perhaps referring to the fish's nest-building habit. *Nuku nuku apuaa* means "nose like a pig." See this beautiful fish at the Waikiki Aquarium in Honolulu.

STATE FLAG

British influence

Hawaii's flag has eight alternating red, white, and blue stripes, one for each of the large islands. The design was adopted by the Hawaiian Kingdom in 1816 following the visit to Hawaii of Captain George Vancouver, successor to Capt. James Cook in exploring the Pacific. The "union jack" in the corner recognizes early rapport between the Hawaiian and British royal families.

STATE FLOWER

Hawaii's most ubiquitous flower

The hibiscus was designated as the official flower of the Territory of Hawaii in 1923 and confirmed as the State flower after statehood in 1959. More than five thousand varieties bloom in Hawaii today.

STATE MAMMAL

Hawaiian breeding grounds

The endangered humpback whale is Hawaii's official marine mammal; fewer than 3,600 remain alive worldwide, of which some 1,500 roam the North Pacific Ocean. An estimated six to seven hundred each winter migrate south to Hawaii's waters to breed and raise their young. They begin to arrive as early as November, but the time to see them is usually late February. The best viewing is in the waters off Maui, but sightings have increased off Kauai, windward Oahu, and the Kona coast of the Big Island. Charter vessels offer whale-viewing cruises in season. Strict federal and State laws restrict close approaches, however.

STATE MOTTO

Ua mau ke ea o ka aina i ka pono

"The life of the land is perpetuated in righteousness" was adopted by the State Legislature in 1959. The phrase originated in an 1843 speech by King Kamehameha III at Kawaiahao Church, Honolulu, after Hawaii's sovereignty was restored by Great Britain.

STATE TREE

Aleurites moluccana

The *kukui* tree replaced the coconut palm as the State tree on May 1, 1959. Its kernels, rich in oil, were strung together by early Hawaiians as a torch, hence its other name, the candlenut tree. Reaching a height of about 45 feet, these trees have conspicuous light yellow-green leaves. Note the greenery on Oahu as you drive across the Nuuanu Pali or tour Manoa or Tantalus; the trees with the lightest (almost yellow) leaves are the kukui. The hard-shelled nuts are strung into distinctive, shiny black leis and jewelry.

Manoa Falls, Oahu

ALOHA

Hawaiian dictionaries include many definitions of "Aloha": a greeting, love, mercy, compassion, farewell and more. Think of *aloha* as meaning welcome to the Islands, an invitation to enjoy our friendly spirit, and warm memories to last a lifetime.

ARCHIPELAGO

The 1,500-mile-long Hawaiian chain consists of 132 islands, reefs, and shoals. The eight largest, with which most people are familiar, are at the southeastern end. The island of Hawaii, known to Hawaii residents as "the Big Island," is the southernmost. Heading northwest, you encounter Kahoolawe, Maui, Lanai, Molokai, Oahu, Kauai, and finally the island of Niihau. These eight islands represent 99.9 percent of the State's total land area of 6,425 square miles. The southern tip of the Big Island is the southernmost point of the United States.

The lesser known Northwestern Hawaiian Islands, totalling only 2.69 square miles of land area, officially are part of the City and County of Honolulu, although the Midway Islands, the largest of this group, are under U.S. Navy control. Kure Atoll, the end of the chain at 28°25' north latitude, 178°25' west longitude, is farthest north. The entire chain beyond Niihau is a federally protected wildlife preserve, and entry is strictly limited.

BEACHES

Papohaku Beach, Molokai

Hawaii's great beaches offer swimming, camping, body-boarding, surfing, wind-surfing, canoeing, kayaking, sailing, snorkeling, scuba diving, and just plain sun worshipping. Water temperatures range between 75° and 80° Fahrenheit all year round.

But even the most inviting beaches in Paradise demand respect—especially during winter. Some, like Oahu's North Shore, are not protected by offshore reefs. Heavy unobstructed surf can not only knock down the unwary, but also pull one out to sea.

The **Big Island**'s Kahaluu Beach Park, just south of Kailua-Kona, is great for kids and beginning snorkelers. So is Hapuna Beach on the South Kohala coast.

Kihei and Wailea on **Maui**'s south shore are famous for their sun and sea, as are Kaanapali, Kapalua, and Fleming's Beach. Hookipa Beach Park, just outside Kahului, does not have much of a beach but it is windsurfer heaven.

On **Kauai**, Poipu Beach on the south side is a favorite. And don't miss Lumahai Beach on the north shore, where *South Pacific* was filmed.

On **Lanai**, Hulopoe Bay offers a perfect South Seas setting. Papohaku and Kawakiu Beaches are Molokai's best.

On **Oahu** (Honolulu), head for Ala Moana Beach Park or familiar Waikiki Beach. Farther east, sheltered and safe Hanauma Bay is a good bet for swimmers and snorkelers. These three locations are particularly popular on weekends and holidays, so get out early for the best spots on the sand.

Makapuu and Sandy Beach at Oahu's eastern end, both premier body-surfing spots, look inviting but are for experienced surfers only. Extreme caution is the price of survival. Lifeguards rescue many unprepared swimmers each year. Don't be one of them! Ask their advice—and follow it.

Kailua, Lanikai, and Waimanalo Beach Parks are your best bets on Honolulu's Windward side.

Please note: alcoholic beverages are prohibited at all beaches.

Heed these safety tips from the U. S. Lifesaving Association, Hawaii region:

- Swim only where a lifeguard is on duty.
- Never swim alone.
- Don't dive into unknown water or into shallow breaking waves.
- Ask the lifeguard about beach and surf conditions before swimming.
- If you are unable to swim out of a strong current, call or wave for help.
- Rely on your swimming ability rather than flotation apparatus.

BIG ISLAND

Residents traditionally call the island of Hawaii, the largest in the Hawaiian Archipelago, "the Big Island." Ninety-three miles long and seventy-six wide, its 4,034 square miles (10,448 square kilometers) account for more than 62 percent of the total land area of the State. Besides possessing the two highest peaks, Mauna Kea (13,796 feet, or 4,205 meters) and Mauna Loa (13,679 feet, or 4,169 meters) the Big Island has the only currently active volcano, Kilauea (hence another nickname, "the volcano isle"). The 32-mile Wailuku River is its longest stream, and Waiakea Pond, all 27 acres of it, is the largest body of fresh water. The Big Island's 130,000 residents account for 11 percent of the State's population.

Because the Big Island provides most of the world's commercially grown orchids, it is often called "the orchid isle." (The island flower, however, is the *lehua*, sacred to Pele, the volcano goddess.) Big Island products include sugar, cattle, macadamia nuts and coffee. The most popular attractions are Kilauea Visitor Center in Hawaii Volcanoes National Park and Lapakahi State Historical Park in the North Kohala district.

BIRDWATCHING

Hawaii Mamo

Isolated in mid-ocean, Hawaii developed a remarkable array of bird species found nowhere else. Regrettably, many have been driven to extinction by habitat destruction, the introduction of predators, and human intrusion. Those that remain usually are elusive.

On the positive side, Hawaii now has a wealth of introduced bird species. Birdwatchers find even a leisurely stroll through Honolulu's Queen Kapiolani Park an exciting experience.

On Oahu, a great place to see forest birds is on the Aiea Loop Trail, at the upper end of Aiea Heights Drive overlooking Pearl Harbor. Shore birds and water birds are usually plentiful around the aqua-culture farms at Kahuku, on the North Shore. Sea birds seem to like the vicinity of the Kaneohe Marine Corps Air Station on the Windward side of the island, but permission to enter the base may be difficult to secure. Failing that, try around Sea Life Park at the extreme eastern end of Oahu.

On the neighboring island of Kauai, visit Kokee State Park for forest birds (including some very rare endemic species), Hanalei Bay for wetland birds, and Kilauea wildlife preserve for the sea birds.

On Maui, the Kahana ponds close to Kahului Airport are locally favored for lowland and water birds. For a view of Hawaii's endemic *nene* goose, as well as several scarce upland species, visit the Haleakala National Park.

The "Big Island" has a wide range of habitats, each with its own bird species. Casual birdwatchers can start at the Kipuka Puaulu, or Bird Park, on the slopes of Mauna Loa above the National Park headquarters at Kilauea. Another good area is in the dryland forest along the Saddle Road between Hilo and Kailua-Kona. Car rental contracts usually forbid driving over that road, however, so alternate transportation is necessary.

Information on birdwatching and conservation matters is available from the Hawaii Audubon Society, 212 Merchant St., #320, Honolulu, HI 96813 (tel. 522-5566).

BOOKS

The University of Hawaii's Hawaiiana collection has 20,000 bound volumes, a good indication of the endlessly fascinating, historically complex saga of Hawaii. The books range from primary source material and reference books to histories, literature and light-hearted contemporary works. In addition, countless illustrated "coffee-table" books star Hawaii's people and scenery.

CAMPING

Camping sites abound in Hawaii: At last count (1985), the Big Island had 824, Oahu (Honolulu) 499, Maui 403, and Kauai 339. Some are run by the National Park Service, others by the State of Hawaii, or one of the four counties. Camping in parks is by permit only; reservations—on a first-come first-served basis—are accepted two to four weeks in advance.

Hawaii has no snakes, skunks, or poison ivy, but it has plenty of mango and Christmas berry, both of which belong to the poison ivy family. Mosquitoes may harass the unprepared camper.Take plenty of insect repellent, mosquito netting for your tent, and mosquito punk. Also be prepared for showers, typically transient but capable of spoiling a nice outing for the underequipped.

Even in Paradise, there are certain human hazards. Be cautious in choosing a camp site. Ask residents for advice on safe areas. Avoid displays of expensive equipment.

CLIMATE See Weather.

COST OF LIVING

Hawaii is one of the most expensive places to live in the United States. Per capita personal income ($21,000 in 1992) exceeds the national average by eleven percent, but not enough to compensate for an estimated 29 percent higher cost of living. But cheer up. Residents save on winter clothing and heating!

CRATERS, CALDERAS AND VOLCANOES

Kilauea fountaining

Although the terms *crater* and *caldera* (Spanish for cauldron) are often used interchangeably, they describe different volcanic features. The great calderas of Hawaii, as elsewhere, were formed by the collapse of volcanic summits. Kilauea caldera, the depressed summit of Kilauea Volcano on the Big Island, is a classic example. You can drive into the shallow basin for a good look at the smaller, deeper Halemaumau Crater within the caldera. Another accessible caldera is the huge erosional depression at the summit of Haleakala on Maui.

Craters are depressions inside calderas or atop volcanic cones. When the lava flow or ash fountaining subsides, the lava drains back into the volcanic "plumbing," leaving a crater inside the built-up cone. Honolulu's Diamond Head, Punchbowl, and Koko Crater are volcanic cinder cones with clearly defined interior craters.

Hawaii's best-known craters and calderas include:

Craters, Calderas and Volcanoes

Island	Area (in acres)	Maximum depth (in feet)
Hawaii		
Kilauea	2,319	476
Mokuaweoweo	2,221	572
(Mauna Loa's summit)		
Maui		
Haleakala	12,575	3,028
Oahu (Honolulu)		
Diamond Head	255	562
Koko Head	133	968
Punchbowl	62	140

CURRENCY

Greenbacks accepted

Standard U.S. currency, travelers' checks, and major credit cards are used. Foreign money can be exchanged at the Honolulu International Airport and at most hotels. Many shops accept Japanese yen, Canadian dollars and other currencies.

DINING (ETHNIC FOOD)

Hawaii is a true "mixing pot" of cuisines. That thick, juicy steak is here, but less familiar delights await the adventurous.

Local Hawaiian fare includes *kalua* pig (roasted in a pit), *laulau* (greens steamed with meat or fish), *lomilomi* salmon (salmon-and-tomato appetizer), *poi* (pounded taro root), and *haupia* (a coconut-based dessert). All can be found at a *luau*, or on a "Hawaiian plate" at a restaurant.

Try spicy Thai cuisine with such exotic names as "Evil Jungle Prince" or "Golden Threads," or Korean *kal-bi* and tangy *kim-chee*. "American food," Cajun, Chinese, Creole, Continental, Filipino, French, Hawaiian, Italian, Japanese, Portuguese, and Vietnamese cooking are within easy reach.

Any visitor information book or the phone book has an eye-opening listing of restaurants. Here are some items on a typical "local" menu:

dim sum - Chinese: "nibble" food, hors d'oeuvres.

haupia - Hawaiian: coconut pudding.

kal-bi - Korean: barbecued beef.

kalua pig - Hawaiian: pork cooked in an underground *imu* oven.

kim chee - Korean: spicy-hot pickled vegetables.

laulau - Hawaiian: fish, pork, and *taro* leaves steamed in a *ti*-leaf pouch. Chicken or beef are often substituted.

9

lomilomi salmon - Hawaiian: salmon mixed with chopped tomatoes and green onions.

luau - A Hawaiian feast.

malasada - Portuguese: doughnuts without holes.

"Plate lunch" - Ubiquitous take-out meal with generous portions of an entree, rice, and salad, served on a paper plate.

poha - Hawaiian: ground cherry. Great as jam or in ice cream!

poi - Hawaiian: *taro* root cooked, pounded, and thinned with water to a thick paste. A starch staple of early Hawaiians, and a must at any authentic luau. *Poi* is fed to infants allergic to milk and soy protein.

sashimi - Japanese: raw fish, typically with a soy sauce-horseradish dip.

shave ice - "Local": flavored finely shaved ice, similar to (but much better than) a snow cone. "Ice shave" in the Big Island's Hilo district.

sushi - Japanese: flavored rice, wrapped with ingredients ranging from vegetables to raw fish, sometimes in dried seaweed.

DIRECTIONS

On an island, landmarks are more practical than compass directions. Instead of east, west, north, and south, Hawaii uses: *"makai"* (toward the ocean), *"mauka"* (toward the mountains), "windward" (northeast, facing the trade winds), and "leeward" (toward the dry southwest side). On Oahu *"ewa"* means to leeward, and "diamond head" is in the direction of that landmark.

DISTANCES

Closest city—San Francisco

Distances of Major Cities from Honolulu

	mi.	km.
Anchorage, Alaska	2,781	4,475
Auckland, N.Z.	4,393	7,068
Brisbane	4,743	7,633
Capetown	11,532	18,559
Chicago	4,179	6,724
Hong Kong	5,541	8,915
London	7,226	11,627
Los Angeles	2,557	4,114
Manila	5,293	8,516
Mexico City	3,781	6,085
Miami	4,856	7,813
Montreal	4,910	7,902
New York City	4,959	7,979
Papeete, Tahiti	2,741	4,410
Paris	7,434	11,964
Portland, Oregon	2,595	4,175
Rio de Janeiro	8,190	13,180
Rome, Italy	8,022	12,910
San Diego	2,610	4,199
San Francisco	2,397	3,857
Seattle	2,679	4,311
Singapore	6,710	10,799
Sydney	5,070	8,158
Tokyo	3,847	6,190
Vancouver, B.C.	2,709	4,359
Washington, D.C.	4,829	7,770
Wellington, N.Z.	4,738	7,625

Distances to Neighbor Islands		
	mi.	km.
Hilo, Hawaii	214	344
Kailua-Kona	168	270
Kahului, Maui	98	158
Lanai Airport	72	116
Molokai Airport	54	87
Lihue, Kauai	103	166

DIVING

Kaanapali, Maui

Just beyond the water's edge is a riot of color—corals, waving sea grass, tentacled and many-legged creatures, and multi-color fish.

Snorkeling and scuba diving offer a peek into this silent, colorful, and very busy world. Visit the Waikiki Aquarium before you head for the beach. It has excellent displays and a shop with helpful guidebooks, as well as waterproof fish-identification cards.

Remember: Never scuba without a knowledgeable "buddy." Tour companies can recommend experienced professional diver-escorts if you are alone or a beginning diver. Most dive shops offer half- and full-day snorkeling and scuba tours—usually in small groups. They usually provide equipment and transportation from your hotel, as well as rental underwater cameras and masks with corrective lenses. Call for details.

Tip: If you are going snorkeling, bring some green peas—yes, peas— to feed the fish. The frozen supermarket kind are easy to carry and the fish love them. But bring the plastic bags ashore afterward, for proper disposal.

On the Big Island, Kahaluu Beach Park, just south of Kailua-Kona, is good for beginning snorkelers. Continue to Kealakekua Bay for real action. (This can involve a lot of swimming, unless you rent a boat. Ask at your hotel or at one of the dive shops.)

Molokini Islet, off the southern (Kihei) beaches of Maui, is for experienced divers. Near Lahaina, Honolua Bay is very good.

Hanauma Bay, on the outskirts of Honolulu, is a busy State marine conservation area where colorful fish have become almost cocky and literally will eat out of your hand. Several companies specialize in Hanauma Bay snorkeling tours.

The island of Kauai also offers some good snorkeling and diving. Ahukini Landing near Lihue town, Kee Lagoon outside Princeville on the north shore, and Old Koloa Landing on the Poipu (southern) side of the island are prime spots.

DRESS

Casual and colorful

Clothingwise, almost anything goes in Hawaii, especially if it's comfortable. "Aloha wear"—a colorful, patterned short-sleeve shirt for men and a long *muumuu* for women—is always in fashion.

A long-running and popular clothing trend has been the decorated Tee-shirt. Emblazoned with anything from flowers to Kliban cats to "I climbed Diamond Head," they are acceptable almost anywhere. Tee-shirts make excellent gifts.

Cool and convenient sandals or rubber slippers (a.k.a. thongs, *zoris* or flipflops) are acceptable wherever your Tee-shirt will go. Don't wear socks with them. You are expected to leave your footwear at the door of most Hawaiian homes, so be prepared.

DRIVING

Yes, left-hand drive is standard here.

Most rental cars take unleaded gas. Leaded gas and diesel fuel are available but sometimes elusive.

The driver and front-seat passenger must wear seat belts. It's the law.

Avoid Honolulu's weekday rush hours—7 to 8:30 a.m. and 3:30 to 6:00 p.m. An open container of alcohol beverage anywhere in a moving vehicle (or in one parked on the street) is an invitation for a police citation. Be prepared for weekend and holiday roadblocks to nab drinkers.

Lock your car and remove valuables WHENEVER you park. Prudence is necessary, even in Paradise.

ECONOMY

Hawaii's gross State product topped $29,324 billion in 1992. Tourism is the State's biggest industry: approximately 6.5 million visitors came in 1992 and spent $10.4 billion.The federal government comes next: the military alone spent $3.2 billion. Agriculture cash sales in 1990 exceeded $500 million (sugar-$270 million, pineapple-$224 million, and flowers-$70 million).

Efforts are being made to diversify by attracting regional corporate headquarters, organizing special sports, cultural and entertainment events, promoting health and fitness activities, encouraging filming for TV and motion pictures, expanding trans-Pacific financial services, and processing and marketing seafood.

FISH AND FISHING

About 680 species of fish call Hawaii home, of which an estimated 420 are classified as reef and shoreline residents. A surprising 30 percent are found nowhere else, a reflection of Hawaii's long isolation from other shores. Many can be seen at the Waikiki Aquarium in Honolulu.

Good fishing and eating

But aside from the *humuhumu-nukunukuapuaa*, the unofficial State fish, the only names you will need are those you want to order for dinner. These include:

Ahi- Yellow-fin tuna. Local deep-sea fishermen love this one for its fighting qualities and for its firm meat. Excellent eating either grilled or raw as *sashimi*.

Aholehole- Silver perch. A tasty wide-eyed night swimmer.

Aku- Striped tuna or skipjack. The major target of commercial tuna fishermen, it also is an excellent game and eating fish. Meat is slightly darker than the ahi.

Mahimahi- The dorado or dolphin fish (not to be confused with the mammalian dolphin, which actually is a porpoise). The skin is a true rainbow of blues, greens, and lavenders that fade to gray when the fish dies. Averaging 17 pounds, but capable of reaching 70, and one of the speediest fish around, they occasionally can be seen flushing and catching flying fish. You can order this all-time favorite anywhere—in a simple "mahi plate" or as a "mahi-burger" (on a hamburger bun) at your neighborhood drive-in, or at the fanciest restaurant where it is served with all the trimmings.

Ono- Wahoo or kingfish.
Opakapaka- Pink snapper.
Onaga- Red snapper.
Ulua- Pampano, giant trevally, or jackfish.

Join Hawaii's many avid fishermen in testing your skill and luck in fresh water, in the surf, on the reef, standing on the shore, or on a charter fishing boat. Ask your hotel tour desk, or look in the yellow pages under "Fishing Parties."

FLORA

Heliconia

With its gentle and varied climate ranging from dry seashores to rain forests, Hawaii is a garden of brilliant flowers, tropical fruit, flowering trees, and exotic greenery.

Many of Hawaii's characteristic flowers and plants were introduced to the Islands by the early Polynesians, who brought breadfruit, banana, mulberry, *taro*, *ti*, and other essential plants. Others, arriving later by ship or by plane, have all but crowded out the approximately 400 indigenous species carried here as seeds by ocean currents and wind, or tucked in the feathers of migrating birds.

Flowers are part of daily life in Hawaii. Prominent in legend and song, floral names are often given to children. Flower motifs adorn the fabrics of men's and women's clothing; fresh flowers are worn in the hair and, of course, are strung together as fragrant *lei*, worn unabashedly by residents on all occasions and presented to visitors. Homes, parks and public buildings in Hawaii are rarely without flowers and plants.

Hawaii's colorful trees, flowers and shrubs are on display in many private and public gardens. Notable gardens are listed in individual island chapters. (See the Flora appendix for a detailed description of some of Hawaii's better known species.)

GEOGRAPHY AND GEOLOGY

The islands of Hawaii were created by volcanic action that began roughly 72 million years ago and continues to this day. Kure Atoll, at the northwestern end of the archipelago, is the oldest remaining island above the sea, but the chain continues northwest-ward, submerged, to within a few hundred miles of Japan. The Big Island at the southeastern end of the 1,600-mile chain is the most recent arrival, but a new island, "Loihi," is slowly building up from the sea bottom to the southeast.

The generally accepted explanation for the island chain's linear arrangement posits a slow, steady northwestward drift of the Pacific Plate over a volcanic "hot spot."

Hawaii's typical landform is a broad, rounded "shield" volcano, built up by innumerable thin lava flows from the ocean floor almost three miles down to heights in excess of two miles above sea level. Mauna Loa on the Big Island is so gentle in its rise that it is difficult to comprehend its 13,600-foot height, which exceeds that of most peaks in the Rockies and the Pacific Coast Range.

Viewing the eight major islands, it is easy to see the geological evolution from the broad swelling shield shapes of the intact "young" volcanoes on the Big Island to the mature, jagged topography of Kauai and the low-lying, heavily eroded remains of an even older shield volcano on Niihau. The volcanic cinder cones, deep valleys, dramatic sea cliffs and broad coastal plains characteristic of older-island topography are the marks of later eruptions and subsequent erosion.

Rainfall causes the most significant erosion. In the case of Waimea Canyon on Kauai, a stream has cut 3,000 vertical feet into the original basalt. Stream erosion is most apparent on the northeast-facing windward sides of the islands, where prevailing winds bring the heaviest rainfall. Windward Oahu, with its near-vertical cliffs and broad valleys, has been so completely transformed by stream action that the original shape of the Koolau shield volcano is difficult to imagine. Leeward slopes, with much less rainfall, show relatively less stream erosion.

Marine erosion, caused by the heavy surf, is most apparent on windward shores. Wind-driven waves have carved 3,000-foot sea cliffs, among the highest in the world, on the north coast of Molokai. Other notable marine cliffs include those along the Hamakua coast of the Big Island and the spectacular Napali cliffs on Kauai.

Sedimentation and reef building combined with changes in sea level over millions of years account for Hawaii's few real "plains." The most notable are along the southwestern shores of Oahu and Kauai. Other forces shaping the land include earthquakes, wind and, of course, man.

GOLF

Golfing paradise

The world recognizes Hawaii as a golfer's paradise, with year-around warm sunny days, steady breezes, and clear skies, all wrapped in an unbelievably blue ocean.That's a fair description most of the time. (Actually, the famous Hawaiian Open tournament had to be recessed once because of too-boisterous trade winds.) Whatever the weather, all but a few of Hawaii's golf courses are well filled all year around.

Kauai has 9 courses with a total of 162 holes, Oahu has 30 courses with 495 holes, Maui 11 courses, with 189 holes, the Big Island 12 courses with 207 holes, rural Molokai two courses, with 27 holes, and Lanai with one nine-hole course. That's a statewide total of 65 courses and 1,089 holes. At least a dozen more courses are under construction or planned.

GOVERNMENT AND POLITICS

At the State Capitol

Hawaii's unusual centralized form of government was shaped by its constitution—written in 1950 in anticipation of statehood and adopted in 1959. There are no cities, towns or school districts, only the State and four counties. The latter—Hawaii (the Big Island), Honolulu (Oahu), Kauai (with neighboring Niihau), and Maui (which takes in Molokai and Lanai)—elect their own "mayors" and "city councils." This is the basis for the sometimes baffling label, "City & County of Honolulu."

An interesting anomaly is Makawao County, a tiny enclave on Molokai Island to accommodate the Kalaupapa leprosy facilities administered by the State Department of Health. It is gradually being phased out, and eventually will be administered entirely by the U.S. National Park Service as Kalaupapa National Historic Park.

Twenty-five senators are elected to the State Legislature every four years, and 51 representatives every two years. The only elective offices in the State administration are the governor and lieutenant governor, both of whom serve four-year terms.

The heads of the 20 State departments and specialized boards are nominated by the governor and confirmed by the State senate.

From the time of U.S. annexation at the turn of the century, Republicans—dominated by local Americans and the "Big Five" businesses—were in control of Hawaii. In 1954, however, with the emergence of strong shipping and plantation workers' unions, and of a well-organized oriental middle class, Democrats took over many key offices, which they have continued to hold. Since 1962, all of Hawaii's governors and a significant majority of its U.S. Congressional delegation (two senators and two representatives) have been Democrats.

Recent years have seen factional struggles within the dominant Democratic Party, several attempts to re-energize the moribund Republican Party, and the rising influence of such special interest groups as labor, business associations, neighborhood boards, the Hawaii Visitors Bureau, Common Cause, the Sierra Club and other environmental groups, the Outdoor Circle, the League of Women Voters, and even a highly vocal Citizens Against Noise. Land-use controversies flare up frequently, involving politicians, bureaucrats, developers, environmentalists, labor unions, and Hawaiian-rights activists.

Probably unique to Hawaii's politics is the charming habit of volunteers gathering at key traffic centers each election season to wave handheld signs (billboards are illegal here) in support of smiling, *lei*-bedecked candidates or ballot issues.

HAWAII VISITORS BUREAU

HAWAII VISITORS BUREAU MARKER

HVB marker

Contact the friendly HVB staff at its offices or booths on all the major islands for help and information. For a copy of *He Kukini* with its calendar of events, facts and suggestions on planning your vacation in Hawaii, write in advance to the main office (2270 Kalakaua Avenue, Suite 801, Honolulu, HI 96813 or telephone (808) 923-1811; Fax 922-8991; Telex 8483 HVB HR). In addition to the main office in Waikiki, the HVB has branches at the Ala Moana Shopping Center in downtown Honolulu, in Hilo and Kailua-Kona on the Big Island, in Lihue on Kauai, and in Wailuku, Maui.

HAWAIIAN AFFAIRS

Although fewer than eight thousand residents are full-blooded Hawaiians (0.8 percent of the State's estimated 1990 population of 1,100,000), part-Hawaiians—the fastest growing population segment—make up almost 20 percent of Hawaii's population. An Office of Hawaiian Affairs (OHA) was constitutionally established in

1979 as a State agency to give Hawaiians a greater voice in government and to coordinate services and programs for them. Nine OHA trustees are elected at-large by voters of Hawaiian extraction.

HELICOPTER TOURS

Enjoying a waterfall, Kauai

Available on almost every island, helicopter tours enable visitors to see the Islands quickly. Flights range in length from six minutes to several hours, and may be expensive. Helicopters can offer spectacular views of otherwise inaccessible places—remote Kalalau Valley, for example, or desolate Niihau, the "forbidden island," or perhaps to an erupting volcano.

HIKING

Great weather and spectacular scenery make Hawaii a natural for hiking. In Honolulu, the Sierra Club (call 538-6616 for a taped message describing the schedule) and the Hawaiian Trail and Mountain Club (P.O.Box 2238, Honolulu, HI 96804; enclose a stamped, self-addressed envelope) have active hiking programs.

Tip: Are you allergic to poison ivy? Watch out for mango and Christmasberry trees. Their resinous sap may provoke the same itchy rash.

HORSEBACK RIDING

Saddle up, stick your feet in the stirrups, and ride off into the hills. Yes, there are horses to ride on all the islands. Look them up under "Stables" in the yellow pages.

HOTELS, RESORTS, BED BREAKFASTS

More than 74,000 hotel rooms and rental apartments await you. Slightly more than half (38,000) are in Honolulu, of which 90 percent are in Waikiki.

Hotel occupancy rates in 1990 ran over 79 percent statewide. Honolulu reported more than 86 percent; Maui 70 percent; Kauai 68 percent; the Big Island 60 percent; and lonely Molokai 48 percent. Whichever island you plan to visit, it's wise to make reservations in advance.

If you arrive in Honolulu without a reservation, look for the lighted hotel-directory panels in the baggage claim lobby of the airport. Many advertise their rates; in any event, use the free phone to inquire. They usually can advise you on the quickest (or cheapest) transportation to their front door.

Valid alternatives to the flashy resorts are the smaller back-from-the-beach hotels and bed-and-breakfast establishments. Accommodations may range from spartan to luxurious, but rates are often very attractive.

The Hawaii Visitors Bureau maintains a fairly extensive register of bed-and-breakfast accommodations. Write ahead for a copy (see Hawaii Visitors Bureau section above for addresses and telephone numbers). In Honolulu, the tastefully restored Manoa Valley Inn,

17

a one-time private home situated in a half acre of shade trees just a block from the University of Hawaii campus, is at the high end ($80 to $145 a night). A room in a private home may be $25 or less.

The other major islands have a similar range of accommodations.

For a description of Hawaii's major accommodations see the Hotels and Resorts appendix.

HULA

Alive and well

An ancient dance form, *hula* was performed by men or women—but rarely together. Men's *hula* was dynamic and active, women's gentle and flowing. The dances were Hawaii's theater, an accompaniment to poetry. Usually dedicated to the goddess Laka, they were part of rites honoring gods and chiefs.

Early missionaries, offended by the scantily clad dancers moving in rhythm to poetry they seldom understood, worked vigorously to abolish *hula*. In the long run, however, they were unsuccessful. In the mid-1800s, King David Kalakaua in particular recognized *hula* as an important aspect of Hawaiian culture and worked to revive it. Today we benefit from his foresight; *hula* is alive and well, and growing in popularity.

Hula competitions are numerous. The biggest is the Merrie Monarch Festival held each April on the Big Island. At Honolulu, the King Kamehameha Competition in June, the Prince Lot Festival in July, and the Queen Liliuokalani Children's Competition in August generate much interest and enthusiasm. "Night club *hula*," while colorful, is strongly influenced by non-Hawaiian forms. Good places for visitors to see modern, authentic *hula* are at the Kodak Hula Show in Kapiolani Park, and the Sunday morning children's "recital" at Ala Moana Center, both in Honolulu.

HURRICANES See Storms.

KAHOOLAWE

Visible on the horizon south of Maui, Kahoolawe is the smallest of the eight major Hawaiian islands. Only eleven miles long and six miles wide, its total area is 45 square miles. The highest point stands 1,483 feet (452 meters). A few feral sheep and goats are the only permanent inhabitants.

Once a spiritual training ground for the Hawaiian priesthood, the *kahuna*, Kahoolawe for forty years has been a U.S. Navy bombing target and war-games staging area. In response to growing opposition to the shelling by Hawaiians who want the island revegetated and ecologically restored, President Bush in 1990 ordered a cease-fire pending final decision.

KAUAI

The "Garden Isle" is the fourth-largest island of Hawaii, measuring thirty-three miles long, twenty-five miles wide and 549 square miles (1,422 square kilometers) in area. About 55,000 residents, nearly 5 percent of the State's total population, live here. Kauai's 5,148-foot Mount Waialeale may be the wettest spot on earth with 444 inches of rainfall a year. Nearby Kawaikini peak is the tallest point on the island at 5,243 feet (1,598 meters). The largest water feature is the 424-acre Waita reservoir, and 19.5-mile Waimea River-Poomau Stream is the longest.

Kauai's most visited cultural attractions are the Russian Fort Elizabeth State Historical Park and the Kokee Natural History Museum. The official island flower is the *mokihana*, a member of the citrus family which produces a fragrant seed used frequently for leis. Tourism and sugar are Kauai's main industries.

KAYAKING

Na Pali coast, Kauai

Kayaking—using either "hard-shell" or inflatable craft—is popular and an excellent way to enjoy Hawaii's surf and sea. Kayak rentals are listed in the yellow pages under "Boat Dealers"; you can arrange kayak tours through your hotel.

KONA WINDS

Winds from the southeast, replacing the usual "trade winds" from the northeast, typically come during winter months and often bring heavy rain and high humidity. The coincidence of names is no reflection on the Big Island's Kona district, which is proud of its beautiful weather.

LANAI

"The Pineapple Island," measuring only eighteen by thirteen miles, with 140 square miles, is sixth in size in the Hawaiian island chain. Lanai City is its only town.

Lanai is governed from Maui. The island's population of slightly more than 2,400 represents about 0.2 percent of the State's total. The main industry used to be growing and shipping pineapples, but tourism is taking over. The island flower is the *kaunaoa*, an orange vine with pointed flowers that are woven into leis.

Like Molokai, until the mid-1980s Lanai was relatively untouched by developers. The few visitors found themselves in another world from Honolulu. Even today, with development a fact of life, Lanai retains the charm of old Hawaii.

In the past, visitors spent the night at the Lanai Hotel, a rustic ten-room lodge with a *lanai* bar and a casual dining room. This is changing. Reorganized and redirected, Castle & Cooke, owner of 98 percent of the island, has built a $260 million resort complex that includes a 102-room "lodge" on a hillside overlooking Lanai City that opened in 1990, a 250-room hotel at Hulopoe Beach, and two golf courses.

LAND USE

Of the 4,112,000 acres in the State, 333,000 are cropland and 974,000 are in pastures. Forest land accounts for 1,473,000 acres, and urban space 126,000 acres. The federal government, including the military, holds 8.4 percent of Hawaii's land; the State and the four counties own 29.8 per cent, and the remaining 61.8 percent is in private hands (a substantial proportion held by large land holding estates).

LEI

Symbol of Aloha

A flower *lei* is the proper greeting for anyone arriving or leaving Hawaii. These garlands are recognized world-wide as fragrant symbols of the Aloha spirit. Worn on the head or around the shoulders, they typically are made of fresh flowers. Leis are worn at celebrations, graduations, weddings, proms, office and home parties, and other happy occasions. Ancient Hawaiians offered leis to the gods, and used them to ward off evil, as symbols of social rank, as personal adornment, and as *hula* wear.

MAUI

Hawaii's second largest island and, next to Oahu, the most visited, Maui "the Valley Island" measures forty-eight miles by twenty-six with 728 square miles (12,887 square kilometers) of land. Haleakala's Red Hill is the third highest point in the State at 10,023 feet (3,055 meters), and Haleakala has the largest crater—12,575 acres.

Some 109,000 people, about 8 per-cent of the State's population, live here. Maui's flower is the *lokelani*, or "heavenly rose." The most popular cultural attractions are Maui Plantation near Wailuku, and the Lahaina Restoration Foundation in Lahaina. Historically an important whaling center, Maui's main industries now are sugar and tourism.

MAY DAY

May Day is Lei Day in Hawaii

May 1 is more than just May Day in Hawaii. It is Lei Day. Each island celebrates with pageants and entertainment at schools, parks, and shopping malls. Of course, the lei plays an integral part in the celebrations. Lei-making contests and demonstrations are held, and the Lei Queen is crowned at Kapiolani Park in Honolulu.

MEDIA

The State's two biggest dailies are the morning *Honolulu Advertiser* and the afternoon *Honolulu Star-Bulletin*. Although they share a building in downtown Honolulu, their ownerships and newsrooms are separate. In addition, the city has one Japanese-and-English daily, one in Korean and one in Chinese.

Kauai, Maui and the Big Island each has one or more papers dealing mostly with local concerns. Honolulu has a network of neighborhood weeklies, magazines and professional periodicals.

The major U.S. television networks have local affiliates: KHON, Channel 2, is NBC; KITV, 4, is ABC; KGMB, 9, represents CBS; and KHNL, 13, is Fox. KHET, Channel 11, and KMEB, Channel 10, are the public television stations.

For a touch of the authentic, tune to KCCN, AM 1420, the "world's only all-Hawaiian music station." For news and sports 24 hours a day, KHVH, AM 990, will keep you filled in. KHPR, FM 88.1, and KKUA, FM 90.7, broadcast National Public Radio shows and classical music. At last count the State had nine commercial and two public television stations, two cable systems, and eighteen AM and eight FM stations with programs ranging from all-news to all-talk, from the classics to rock and country-western, primarily in English but including programs in Japanese, Korean, Chinese, Hawaiian, Samoan and the Philippine dialects.

MEDICAL

Hawaii is not only a great place to be (one survey ranked it number one nationwide) but is one of the ten healthiest in the nation also. Male life expectancy is 75.3 years. For females it is 80.92 years. People here are less overweight, and are more active.

Health facilities include twenty-five acute-care hospitals with 3,175 beds, forty long-care facilities (3,416 beds), and eleven specialty establishments (1990 figures).

MICHENER'S *HAWAII*

Certainly one of the most widely read books about Hawaii, James A. Michener's tidal wave of a novel covers the islands from their creation 30 million years ago to 1957. First published in 1959 and reprinted almost annually ever since, *Hawaii* dramatizes the Islands' geography, people, and destiny, tracing the journeys from all over the world of those who now call Hawaii home.

Hawaii's main characters, institutions, and some events are fictional, but their stories are told in the context of actual Hawaiian history. Thirty years after its publication, James Michener's *Hawaii* remains one of the best introductions to Paradise, dramatizing the State's uniqueness.

MILITARY

At Pearl Harbor

In 1991, some 54,000 officers and enlisted men of the U.S. Army, Navy, Air Force, Marines and Coast Guard (including 2,600 aboard ships) and 63,000 military dependents were stationed in Hawaii, representing about 10 percent of Hawaii's population and a significant portion of the State's income. The importance of the military in Hawaii is indicated by the following: total expenditures, $2.6 billion (defense is second only to tourism as a source of Hawaii's income); prime contract awards, $512 million; civilian employees, 20,000; veterans in civilian life, 100,000; retired military personnel, 10,900 (receiving $13.5 million monthly); military dependents attending public schools, 20,100; military housing, 19,400 units; land owned or controlled by the armed services, more than 265,000 acres.

Military Bases and Personnel by Installation or Area (1990)

	Military	Civilian
Aiea	479	283
Barbers Point	1,480	371
Ford Island	330	35
Fort Shafter	2	2,033
Hickam Air Force Base	5,763	1,942
Honolulu	1,627	356
Kaneohe	4,574	687
Kapalama	30	183
Kauai	150	137
Kunia	1,505	49
Lualualei	213	268
Pearl Harbor	7,426	10,051
Schofield Barracks	13,616	1,098
Tripler Army Medical Center	–	1,361
Wahiawa	730	182
Wheeler AFB	880	462
Other	179	359
State Total	**39,936**	**19,857**

Source: The 1992 State of Hawaii Data Book

MISSIONARIES

Mission Houses Museum

When the first westerners arrived, they found no Hawaiian writing system. Early American missionaries developed a Hawaiian alphabet, based on English sounds which sometimes differed from the Hawaiian, and put spoken Hawaiian into written form. Their printing presses produced Bibles, textbooks, and newspapers in Hawaiian. They rapidly established schools, initially to teach religion but which before long taught many nonreligious subjects. The same missionaries also introduced Western medicine and encouraged the development of agriculture and manufacturing, giving Hawaii an economic base for trade. Nearly 20,000 Hawaiians converted to Christianity between 1837 and 1840.

Although Congregational missionaries from New England took the early lead, other nations, other denominations, and other creeds were also active. Catholicism was introduced by France in 1839 (despite Protestant-inspired efforts to keep it out) and the Anglican Church (Episcopalian) was invited in two decades later. With the arrival of Chinese, Korean and Japanese plantation workers, Buddhism, Confucianism, Taoism, and Shinto followed. Today, practically every religious persuasion is represented in the Islands.

MOLOKAI

The "Friendly Island," Molokai is about midway in size (fifth) in the Hawaiian chain, being thirty-eight miles long and ten wide, with 260 square miles of land area. Its tallest peak is Kamakou, 4,961 feet (1,512 meters). Wailua-Pulena Stream, the longest, runs only 6.5 miles. But Molokai has the tallest waterfall in the State, Kahiwa Falls, with a 1,750-foot cascade. Kaunakakai is the largest town. All government functions are handled from Maui. The island flower is the kukui.

With the highest concentration of Hawaiians outside Niihau, these neighborly people cling to a more traditional way of life. Visitors are relatively few. Total population is 6,700.

Pineapple no longer is Molokai's life. Dole shut down its plantation in 1975. Del Monte followed in 1988, forcing both residents and government to take a hard look at Molokai's future.

Hawaiian activists, concerned with preserving the island's unique life style, have fought developers "who want to turn Molokai into another Waikiki." A tacit compromise accepts the west end, already dominated by the 6,700-acre Kaluakoi Resort, as the only major target for tourism growth. The east end is to be preserved as it is today.

MONARCHY

From 1795 to 1893, Hawaii was an independent monarchy. A celebrated warrior and shrewd diplomat, Kamehameha I ("the Great") progressively overcame the other island chiefdoms in the decade following the visit by Captain Cook in 1777 (the island of Kauai held out until 1810) and peaceably ruled the unified Hawaiian nation until his death in 1819.

Queen Kaahumanu

Kamehameha the Great

The nephew of a Big Island chief, Kamehameha won control of the island of Hawaii in 1790. Two young Caucasian seamen, John Young and John Palmer Parker (family names still prominent in Hawaiian affairs; see the section dealing with the Parker Ranch in the Island chapter that follows) joined Kamehameha to handle recently introduced guns and cannons. By 1795, Kamehameha had subdued Maui, Molokai, and Oahu. In the decisive battle for Oahu, two fleets of war canoes, led by Kamehameha, landed at Waikiki and Waialae (Honolulu), and drove the Oahu forces up Nuuanu Valley. The defenders made an unsuccessful stand above the cliffs of the Nuuanu Pali. Trapped, they either surrendered or were pushed off

the precipice. Thereafter, Kamehameha was the undisputed monarch of all the islands except Kauai and Niihau. The Kauai chief, Kaumualii, made peace with Kamehameha in 1810, and Hawaii thereafter was united.

Kamehameha not only united the islands but also firmly led them into the modern world. While maintaining the religion of his ancestors, he sought advice and new ideas from westerners who arrived in increasing numbers during his reign. Twice he diplomatically defended the kingdom against Russian military intervention, and he encouraged foreigners to set up businesses and trade. After his death, Kamehameha's bones were secretly hidden; their whereabouts are unknown to this day. A heroic (and idealized) statue of the great king stands in front of Aliiolani Hale, the State judiciary building in downtown Honolulu. A copy (actually, the original) has been erected near his birthplace

Liholiho, Kamehameha II

on the north shore of the Big Island.

Two sons, Liholiho (Kamehameha II, 1796-1824) and Kauikeaouli (Kamehameha III, 1813-1854), and two grandsons, Alexander Liholiho (Kamehameha IV, 1834-1863) and Lot Kapuaiwa (Kamehameha V, 1830-1872) followed him to the throne before the family line died out.

Kamehameha III and Queen Kalama

Western influence increased dramatically after unification. Liholiho and his foster mother, Queen Kaahumanu (Kamehameha's favorite wife), abolished the ancient *kapu* system of ritual taboos, and embraced Christianity. American Protestant missionaries became the royal family's closest advisers and helped lay the groundwork for a constitutional government in the 1840s. France and England both tried to influence the royal family, and the fourth Kamehameha, Alexander Liholiho, embraced Anglicanism.

Alexander Liholiho, Kamehameha IV

Lot Kapuaiwa, Kamehameha V

Three elected monarchs followed the Kamehameha line: William Charles Lunalilo (1833-1874); David Kalakaua (1836-1891); and Lydia Kamakaeha Kaolamalii Liliuokalani (1838-1917).

The reign of David Kalakaua, the "Merrie Monarch," marked the high point of an extravagant monarchy. The son of a high chief, Kalakaua won the throne in 1874 and reveled in the trappings of royalty. On a tour of Europe, kings and queens received him as an equal. On his return to Honolulu, he built Iolani Palace and had himself crowned in a lavish ceremony that combined the traditions of the Hawaiian alii with Victorian pomp and pageantry. He visited Washington, D.C., where he negotiated an economically vital reciprocity treaty with the United States. But at home, Kalakaua's flamboyance and his sometimes corrupt companions caused increasing unrest among Honolulu's powerful sugar growers (many of them missionary descendants) and their business allies. In 1887, a particularly nasty scandal forced the king to sign the "Bayonet Constitution", which stripped him of most of his power and denied voting rights to two-thirds of the native Hawaiians. Kalakaua died four years later on a trip to San Francisco.

Today Kalakaua is remembered as a king whose hearty love for Hawaiian music and hula kept his people's culture alive during a stolid and disapproving Victorian era. He was the beloved Merrie Monarch, a man who brought dazzling gaiety to the hard lives of his subjects.

David Kalakaua, "Merrie Monarch"

Queen Liliuokalani, Hawaii's last reigning monarch, was musically accomplished and composed much of Hawaii's most beautiful music, including "Aloha Oe." Her strength and dignity during the bitter last years of the monarchy have made her a fondly remembered figure in Hawaiian history. Her statue stands at the State capitol in downtown Honolulu.

Iolani Palace, built by Kalakaua

Liliuokalani struggled to restore the power of the monarchy lost by her brother Kalakaua, but her efforts increased resentment against the monarchy, particularly by businessmen who sought annexation by the United States. In a bloodless coup in 1893, the monarchy was overthrown. Liliuokalani was imprisoned in her palace, and the Kingdom of Hawaii became the Republic of Hawaii with a provisional government led by annexationist Sanford B. Dole. Five years later, in 1898, at the height of American expansion during the Spanish-American War, Hawaii was annexed by the United States.

Queen Liliuokalani

MOPEDS

Handy motorized scooters are one of the least expensive ways to get around. Moped rentals by the hour, day, or week are available on all major islands.

While driving a moped, remember to wear bright clothing, turn on the headlight even during the day to increase your own visibility to oncoming drivers (don't forget to turn it off), and follow all safety rules. Keep off the freeways!

MUSIC

The Brothers Cazimero

That unforgettably beautiful and haunting blend of mellow voices, rising and falling in harmony with a *ukulele*, guitar, bass and steel guitar that characterizes Hawaiian music evolved over the years as contacts with the West increased.

The guitar arrived from Mexico and California with early whalers and traders. Hawaiians took the standard guitar one step further with the "slack key" style. What was to become the *ukulele* came later with the Portuguese. The bass and the steel guitar were added, rounding out the familiar group of instruments you hear today in much contemporary Hawaiian music.

The *kahiko* chants of old Hawaii are a far cry from today's lilting refrains. After the missionaries introduced western-style melody and harmony with their hymns, Heinrich Berger, German-born conductor of the Royal Hawaiian Band during the reign of Kamehameha V, was a major influence, composing 75 of his own songs, and arranging more than a thousand Hawaiian songs.

NIIHAU

It would have been easier for Captain Cook to visit Niihau Island in 1778 than for curious outsiders to do so today. The low, arid seventy-three square-mile "forbidden island" is *kapu*, off limits, to everyone except its 300 or so Hawaiian residents and guests of its owners, the Robinson family of Kauai.

Visible from Kauai's west side, and legally part of Kauai County, Niihau lies in the lee of Kauai's mountains which block the trade-wind rain clouds that keep the Garden Isle green.

Niihauans raise cattle and sheep, make charcoal from thorny *kiawe* trees, cultivate bees, and pick up tiny, colorful sea shells to string into Niihau shell leis, treasured by women of Hawaii and proudly worn at social functions.

In its isolation, Niihau retains a perhaps unmatched spirit of old Hawaii. Hawaiian remains the common language. An intact rural lifestyle is tied more closely to the nineteenth century than to the twenty-first.

OAHU

Forty-four miles long and thirty miles wide, Oahu is the third largest of the Hawaiian islands, with 593 square miles (1,537 square kilometers). The usual translation of the name, "the gathering place," is appropriate since nearly 77 percent of the State's population (civilian) lives here.

The original attraction was Honolulu's sheltered anchorage. The tallest mountain is 4,017-foot (1,224-meter) Mount Kaala in the Waianae Range. The wettest spot is the Lyon Arboretum in Honolulu's Manoa Valley with 158 inches of rain a year. Thousand-acre Kawainui Marsh on the Windward side is the largest body of water, and the longest stream is the 33-mile south fork of Kaukonahua Stream flowing across the Schofield Plateau to the North Shore.

Oahu's most visited attractions are the National Cemetery of the Pacific (the Punchbowl) and the U.S.S. *Arizona* Memorial at Pearl Harbor.The island flower is the *ilima*. Major industries are tourism, the federal government, and agriculture.

The City and County of Honolulu (a single entity) covers the entire island.

"PIDGIN ENGLISH"

Although commonly called "pidgin English," Hawaii's widely used and often amusing patois is technically a "creole" language. Using words of English, Hawaiian and other origins, it developed as a common language among immigrant plantation workers from many parts of the world. Today, most island-born residents use "pidgin" and standard English inter-changably, often mixing them unself-consciously for emphasis. Here are a few words and phrases that you may overhear:

Broke da mouth (brok da mout)- Tastes great.

Chicken skin (CHEEken skeen)-Goose bumps.

Cockaroach (Kaka-roach)-To steal or take.

Da kine (daKINE)-Generic fill-in-the-blank word comparable with "whatchamacallit and "thingamajig."

Grind (GRINE)-To eat.

Grinds (GRINES)-Food.

Howzit (HOWzit)?-How are you?

Humbug (HUMbug)-Bother; nuisance.

Junk-Not very good.

Kaukau (COWcow)-Food.

Mahalo plenty (maHAlo)- Many thanks.

Max Out-To overdo something.

Mo bettah (mo BEHdah)- Much better, or just better.

Nah-Just kidding.

No mention (no MENchun)- Don't mention it.

Pau hana (pow HAna)- Quitting time (from work).

Real ono (reel OHno)-Tastes great!

Shaka (SHAH ka)-Right on! Always accompanied by a hand gesture (thumb and little finger up, middle three fingers down). The gesture also means "Howzit."

Suck 'em up-Drink up.

Talk story (talk STAHee)- Shoot the breeze; exchange stories; converse.

T'anks eh? Thank you.

To da max-To the limit.

PINEAPPLES

Still popular

No one knows when the first pineapple arrived in Hawaii. It was not brought by early Polynesians. However, it was here by January 21, 1813, when Don Francisco Marin made a casual entry in his diary about planting one.

A vital part of the Hawaiian economy for many years now, pineapple had a rather shaky start. The first two attempts at commercial planting in the mid-to-late 1800s failed. It took the arrival of James D. Dole in 1899 to start the industry rolling. He established large plantations and built a cannery right next to the fields, producing his first commercial "pack" in 1903. Pineapple has since become inextricably associated with Hawaii.

Sharply increased production costs and foreign competition have eroded the importance of pineapple, although it still (1990) contributes $216 million to the State's economy. Hawaiian "pine" remains popular worldwide despite the competition, because it is delicious.

Unfortunately, badly needed housing has begun to fill the broad, open pineapple fields that once characterized Hawaii's scenery. But Oahu and Maui still have large plantations worth a visit.

Tips on Pinapples:
• Fresh pineapples from Hawaii are picked at maximum ripeness for delivery to U.S. and Canadian markets. A pineapple will not ripen further or get any sweeter after picking. The sugar comes from conversion of starch reserves in the stump at the time of ripening. Also, shell color is not necessarily a sign of maturity or ripeness. A practically green pineapple may be ripe. The sooner pineapples are eaten, the better. If you do not plan to use a fresh pineapple right away, store it in the refrigerator. It will keep better and longer.
• Fresh pineapple contains bromelain, an enzyme that breaks down protein. Because of this, gelatin made with pineapple will not set. Cottage cheese and other diary products should not be mixed with fresh pineapple until just before serving.
• You can use fresh pineapple in a meat marinade to add an accent and to help tenderize tough cuts.

POLYNESIA

Polynesia is the most widely scattered of the three island groups (the other two are Micronesia and Melanesia) that make up Oceania, the overall term for the island cultures of the south and central Pacific Ocean.

Polynesia is huge and roughly triangular, with New Zealand in the southwest corner, Easter Island in the southeast, and the Hawaiian Archipelago at the apex in the north.

Within the group are the Samoan Islands, Tonga, the Society Islands (Tahiti), the Marquesan group, the Tuamotu archipelago, the Mangareva Islands, and the Cook Islands.

Bora Bora, French Polynesia

The people of Polynesia share many genetic, linguistic, social, material, and religious characteristics. Anthropologists now suspect that a single, consistent migration from central Melanesia and Micronesia into Tonga and Samoa began about 1000 B.C. and continued, without interference from other ethnic groups, up until A.D. 500, resulting in the settlement of the Society Islands, the Marquesas, Easter Island, Hawaii, and New Zealand.

Essential to the wide dispersal of the Polynesians were ocean-going outrigger canoes unique to their culture. In these craft, the Polynesians traveled greater distances than any other seafarers of the time. Polynesian navigational skills, based on direct observation of ocean, wind and currents, weather patterns, stars, and migrations of sea birds, are still not fully understood by modern scientists.

With their handsome appearance and natural friendliness, Polynesians have long appealed to westerners. For many, Polynesia was the perfect antidote to the complexities, pieties, and vain sophistications of European civilization. It has offered refuge to such sensitive romantics as Paul Gauguin, Robert Louis Stevenson and others exhausted by western life.

Today's Hawaii, with its high rises, freeways, and ubiquitous fast-food outlets, may seem to have shed its Polynesian heritage. But look around. *Hula*, surfing, and outrigger-canoe racing—Polynesian activities—are still popular. The importance of the extended family in Polynesian culture is evident in the large gatherings of local folks at beach picnics, elaborate baby

Moorea, Tahiti

luau (on the occasion of a first birthday), and clan reunions. The ceremonial use of flowers is distinctly Polynesian, as is the remarkable durability of the aloha spirit, that special local friendliness that defies analysis.

POPULATION/PEOPLE

"Rainbow" is a word heard often in discussions of Hawaii's people. Hawaii has no single ethnic majority. Everyone in Hawaii is a member of a minority, and many are several minorities mixed together. About 29 percent of Hawaii's marriages in 1990 were interracial, further proof of the amazing racial assimilation going on since native Hawaiians first welcomed foreigners to their shores.

After "discovery" by European explores in the late eighteenth century, merchants, sailors, missionaries, fortune hunters, and adventurers from all over the world came to Hawaii. Many stayed and married. The rise of large sugar and pineapple plantations and subsequent labor shortages in the late nineteenth and early twentieth centuries brought in thousands of Chinese, Japanese, Portuguese and Filipino workers, most of whom stayed when their labor contracts expired. Many single men married local Hawaiian women. Japanese women were early arrivals, reflected in the distinctive strength and uniformity of the Japanese community in Hawaii. This homogeneity, however, is breaking down today as third-and fourth-generation Japanese marry.

Filipinos, both men and women, have arrived in strength, particularly since World War II. They have established themselves as an important element of the community.

Hawaii continues to add new shades to its racial rainbow as Samoans, Tongans, Koreans, Vietnamese, and Cambodians arrive. Wealthy Japanese and "refugees" from the continental U.S. come as well, ready to pay top dollar for their niche in Paradise.

	TOTAL	Oahu	Hawaii	Kauai	Maui
Unmixed					
White	250,102	189,382	29,005	8,679	23,036
Japanese	241,637	190,176	25,810	9,842	15,809
Chinese	50,138	47,912	1,446	247	533
Filipino	117,471	84,034	10,703	10,362	12,372
Hawaiian	10,962	5,424	2,989	510	2,039
Korean	11,892	11,001	126	116	649
Black	20,656	20,362	174	35	85
Puerto Rican	3,311	2,217	565	180	349
Samoan	6,249	6,249			
Other	12,536	10,562	550	297	1,127
All Groups	**724,954**	**567,319**	**71,918**	**30,268**	**55,999**
Mixed					
Part Hawaiian	199,776	138,695	27,792	10,275	23,024
Non-Hawaiian	119,301	90,172	13,785	5,681	9,663
Total	**319,007**	**228,857**	**41,577**	**15,956**	**32,687**

Source: The 1992 State of Hawaii Data Book

This class of girls, taken at one of Honolulu's schools for girls in or before the 1920s, shows how cosmopolitan Hawaii's population had become. This trend continues today with almost half of all marriages being inter-racial.

1. Hawaiian **2.** Ehu Hawaiian **3.** Japanese **4.** Chinese **5.** Korean **6.** Russian **7.** Filipino **8.** Portuguese **9.** Polish-Russian **10.** Hawaiian-German **11.** Hawaiian-Chinese **12.** Hawaiian-Russian **13.** Hawaiian-American **14.** Hawaiian-French **15.** Hawaiian-Portuguese **16.** Hawaiian-Filipino-Chinese **17.** Hawaiian-Indian-American **18.** Hawaiian-Japanese-Portuguese **19.** Hawaiian-Portuguese-American **20.** Hawaiian-Spanish-American **21.** Hawaiian-German-Irish **22.** Hawaiian-Spanish-German **23.** Hawaiian-Chinese-American **24.** Hawaiian-Portuguese-Irish **25.** Hawaiian-Japanese-Indian **26.** Hawaiian-Portuguese-Chinese-English **27.** Hawaiian-Chinese-German-Norwegian-Irish **28.** South Sea (Nauru)-Norwegian **29.** African-French-Irish **30.** Spanish-Puerto-Rican **31.** Guam-Mexican-French **32.** Samoan-Tahitian

If there is an emerging, dominant ethnic group it is the children of racial intermarriages who count a handful of different nationalities in their blood. Hawaii is not far from the day when its native-born residents will be unable to designate themselves as members of any one racial group. If asked their racial background, they might say, "Well, I'm from Hawaii and, uh, what was the question?"

Chinese

There is a story that the Chinese were in Hawaii before Captain Cook. They began to arrive in large numbers between 1852 and 1856, when several thousand came as plantation laborers. The majority were men from the Pearl River delta near Hong Kong and Macao. Many married Hawaiian women. Chinese-Hawaiian families today are prominent in business and politics.

Like the immigrant groups that arrived after them, hardworking and astute Chinese headed for Honolulu to open their own businesses once they had fulfilled their indentured labor contracts. The Islands had a Chinese population of some 6,000 in 1878, and more than 18,000 by 1884. By last count, the 49,000 who listed themselves as ethnically Chinese represented 5 percent of the State's population.

Filipinos

The last of the large-scale immigrant labor groups, nearly 20,000 Filipinos—mostly Tagalogs, Visayans, and Ilocanos—arrived between 1907 and 1931. Like the Chinese, Japanese and other groups before them, Filipinos moved upward after their labor contracts expired and are now an integral part of Hawaii's mainstream. Although some returned to the Philippines with their savings, Filipinos now constitute more than 11 percent of Hawaii's population.

Haole (Caucasians)

The first recorded contact between Hawaiians and westerners occurred on January 20,1778, when British Captain James Cook and his men landed on the island of Kauai. Journals and sketches by his officers brought the Islands to the attention of European and American officials, traders and whalers. Hawaiians called these early arrivals *haole*s, a term of uncertain derivation. Today the word refers to Caucasians in general, except Portuguese (see below), whether old-timers or newcomers.

In the 1820s, Protestant New England missionaries arrived in Hawaii to administer to the spiritual needs of the whalers—and to convert Hawaiians. French Roman Catholic, American Mormon, and British Anglican missionaries followed, but the New Englanders, closely allied with whalers and merchants, predominated and became important advisers to Hawaiian kings. Although 1853 census figures showed only 1,887 Caucasians, their political and economic influence far exceeded their numbers. By 1898, the year Hawaii was annexed as a U.S. territory, roughly 20 percent of the population was white.

Since World War II, immigration from the continental U.S. has raised the white, nonmilitary, resident population to 239,000, about 23 percent of the State's population.

Hawaiians

Archaeological and linguistic evidence indicates that Hawaii was settled in two phases. The first group arrived from the Marquesan Islands, at least by A.D. 600 or 700 and perhaps as early as the first century, while the second wave came about A.D. 1100 from the Society Islands. Making these immense voyages across vast expanses of empty water was no small feat. A major contribution to the success of these trips was the 80 to 100-foot Polynesian double canoes, consisting of two hulls with a platform lashed between them to provide space for cooking, storage, and living during the long voyages. Polynesians were remarkable navigators, traversing thousands of miles guided only by their knowledge of the sky, the stars, the sea and its currents, and the birds and other natural signs.

Voyaging back and forth initially, these early pioneers eventually settled in their new land and lost contact with southern Polynesia. Isolated for centuries, some of their ways changed as they adapted to their new home; what emerged was a unique culture.

Only 9,417 people in the State are considered to be pure Hawaiian. Almost 20 percent, 203,355, however, classify themselves as part-Hawaiian.

Japanese

Although they first arrived in 1868, the Japanese did not come in large numbers until 1886. Like the Chinese, they came as contract laborers to work on the plantations. Unlike the Chinese, more men came with their wives and children, and single men sent home for "picture brides." This kept inter-marriage to a minimum.

Once their contracts were fulfilled, Japanese moved on to become trades-men and small businessmen. These *issei*, "first generation," typically made great financial sacrifices to insure their children's success. With the advantage of a western educa-tion their parents seldom had, the *nisei*, "second generation," took pro-fessional or white-collar jobs. By 1890 more than 12,000 Japanese were in Hawaii, growing to more than 61,000 by 1900. In the early 1900s, almost 40 percent of the island population was Japanese. Today they number over 235,000, or 23 percent.

Koreans

The first major group of Koreans reached Hawaii in 1903 aboard the S.S. *Gaelic*. During the next few years, 7,843 more arrived. Then in 1905, the government of Korea stopped labor emigration, citing rumors of ill-treat-ment of Koreans in Mexico. A recent count numbered 13,284 in Hawaii, ap-proximately 1.3 percent of the State's population.

Portuguese

Although the Far East contributed most of the labor recruited to Hawaii's plantations in the late 1800s, some workers came from Europe. Portu-guese, mostly from the Atlantic is-lands of Madeira and the Azores, made up the largest number. Only 486 Portuguese were in Hawaii in 1878. Of the 17,500 contract work-ers recruited, most arrived in the next eight years. Portuguese were also ea-ger to leave the plantations once their contracts expired, and many went into business. Today, almost 7 percent of the State's population claims Portu-guese ancestry.

1. Samoan girls
2. A man of Polynesian ancestry
3. Japanese girl
4. A Korean dancer
5. Potpourri of Hawaii's children
6. Hawaiian boy

RAINFALL

Hawaii's rainfall varies considerably within each island and between seasons. The wettest spot in the State (and possibly the world) is Mount Waialeale on Kauai, which gets an average of 444 inches of rain a year. Honolulu's Lyon Arboretum in Upper Manoa Valley, averaging 158 inches, is Oahu's wettest. Kawaihae on the Big Island is the driest spot in the State with only 8.7 inches a year.

November through March tend to be the wettest in Honolulu, with monthly rainfall usually 2.72 to 3.79 inches. The driest season is June through September, when the range is from 0.49 to 0.62 inches. In 1988, Honolulu had only 100 days with 0.01 inches or more precipitation. That meant 268 clear or mostly clear days, giving you a 73 percent chance for excellent weather!

SAILING AND CRUISES

Go eye to eye with fishy friends aboard a glass-bottom boat. Dance over the waves under billowing sails. Take an all-day sailing and swimming tour. Or pamper yourself with a sunset dinner cruise under a full moon. You can find the right cruise for you and your pocketbook from your hotel tour desk or by looking in the yellow pages under "Boats- Charter" or "Boats-Sightseeing Trips."

SHELL COLLECTING

Malacological delights

Many of Hawaii's seashells, tree snails and terrestrial species are found nowhere else. The State's spectacular tiger and checkered cowries are famous.

Casual collecting is best done with snorkel, mask and flippers. On Oahu, the shallow reefs off the Ala Moana end of Waikiki, around Magic Island, and off Ala Moana Beach Park are the habitat of many common shells. More adventuresome shellers might try Windward Oahu's fringing reefs, particularly at the Kaaawa, Hauula and Punaluu Beach Parks, or near the Crouching Lion Inn. When the surf permits, Alii Beach Park at Haleiwa on the North Shore frequently is productive.

Over-collecting is a constant threat to Hawaii's molluscs. Limit your "bag." And turn rocks and coral back after you have looked under them.

The Hawaiian Malacological Society, P.O. Box 22130, Honolulu, HI 96823-2130, publishes an interesting and informative monthly, *Hawaii Shell News*. The Bernice P. Bishop Museum has a world-class study collection of Pacific tree snails. Telephone 847-3511 in advance to see it.

SKIING

Mauna Kea, island of Hawaii

Believe it or not, in winter there is snow skiing on Mauna Kea on the Big Island! The mountain has fast, hard-packed corn snow, no trees, runs as long as five miles, and no waiting for a seat on a lift! As a matter of fact, it has no lifts either, no ski classes, no powder snow, and no nightlife. Access is by four-wheel drive or helicopter.

STORMS

True hurricanes, cyclonic storms with winds in excess of 72 miles an hour, seldom reach Hawaii, but when they do, the results can be devastating. On September 11, 1992, Hurricane Iniki, with sustained winds of 145 mph and gusts topping 175 mph, hit Kauai and brushed the Waianae Coast of Oahu, causing five deaths and billions of dollars in damage.

SUGAR

Acres of sweet green

Sugar cane was one of the food plants brought to Hawaii by the early Polynesians. In his journal, Captain Cook mentions seeing it in Hawaiian gardens.

Not until the American Civil War brought skyrocketing sugar prices in the mid-1860s did the Hawaiian sugar industry gain importance. By 1866, Hawaii was exporting almost 18 million pounds of sugar a year.

As the industry grew, a severe labor shortage developed and foreigners were invited in. After their contracts expired, many workers stayed to join the diverse "melting pot" of races for which Hawaii has become famous. Descendants of these immigrants now are among Hawaii's leaders.

In recent years, sugar has diminished in importance although in 1991 it still contributed $271 million to the State's economy.

Recent bad storms and their tolls:

"Hiki"	August 1950	68 mph	$200,000
"Della"	Sept. 1957	82 mph	minor
"Nina"	Nov.-Dec.1957	92 mph	1,057,000
"Dot"	August 1959	81 mph	5,500,000+
"Fico"	July 1978	58+ mph	188,000
"Iwa"	Nov. 1982	100+ mph	234,000,000
"Iniki"	Sept. 1992	145+ mph	2,000,000,000+

Sugar is also important to Hawaii's natural beauty. Formerly dry but fertile land became broad green cane fields, thanks to advances in irrigation and growing techniques pioneered by the sugar industry.

SURFING

'Sport of Kings'

Welcome to Hawaii, with its 1,600 recognized surfing sites! Of these, Oahu has 594, Kauai 330, Maui 212, and the Big Island 185. Surfboards and racks adorn car roofs everywhere. Rear window decals proclaim favorite surf shops. Surfers are in the water before dawn, after dusk, and at every hour of the day. Surfing may not be a religion here, but it is a recognized substitute.

Hawaiians were surfing long before Captain Cook arrived in 1778, but it took the great Olympic Gold Medal swimmer Duke Kahanamoku to introduce this ancient "sport of kings" to the mainland United States and Australia. During summer, the south shores of all the islands get the best waves. If you want to see really awesome surf, come during winter to marvel at the body and surfboard crushers that pound Oahu's North Shore in "sets" (surf) towering 25 feet or more. Call 836-1952 for the surf report.

SWELLS

Swells are large ocean waves that move steadily without breaking until they reach land. The best for surfing are generated by Antarctic or North Pacific storms, and travel thousands of miles. As they get close to shore, the progressively shallower bottom or a reef causes them to rise, eventually breaking and creating some of the best surf in the world.

TANNING

Start off slowly

Foolish people come to Hawaii for a tan, unaware (or disdainful) that the potent tropical sun can roast them while they are hunting for their skin lotion. Dermatologists recommend that everyone apply a sunscreen with a minimum SPF (sun protective factor) of 15 before going outdoors. Suffering from a bad sunburn is *not* the way to enjoy Hawaii. Be especially careful to avoid falling asleep on the beach, even on a cloudy day; 80 percent of the devastating ultraviolet light that prematurely ages your skin and causes skin cancer comes right through the clouds. Some of the worst sunburns are received on cloudy days. No amount of expensive unguent will restore your smooth skin. Above all, your smooth skin. Above all, do not expect tanning oils or butters to protect you; they literally allow the sun to fry you.

TAXIS

The meters on Honolulu cabs (1992) begin at $1.50, with an additional charge of $1.65 per mile. Rates vary between islands and areas.

Downtown Honolulu is four to five miles from central Waikiki. A taxi ride from the airport to Waikiki costs about $15, with an additional charge for baggage.

Tip: Inexpensive city bus service in Honolulu covers the entire island.

TENNIS

Courts with a view at Wailea, Maui

Tennis courts, both indoors and out, abound in this State, where the game is more a way of life than a sport. Of the 278 public statewide courses, Oahu (Honolulu) has 174 at 46 facilities.

TIME

You will hear references to "Hawaiian time." That means "approximately." Don't be upset by tardiness. Enjoy it.

Hawaii does not change to Day-light Saving Time when the rest of the nation does. During the summer when our clocks say noon, it is 3:00 p.m. on the West Coast, and 6 p.m. in Manhattan.

From October to April, when the rest of the country is back on Standard Time, 12:00 in Hawaii is 2 p.m. in Hollywood and 5 p.m. in Brooklyn.

TOURS

Tours of all kinds abound. Check at your hotel, or find them in the yellow pages under the following categories:

•**Catamaran cruises**: Look under "Boats-Charter."
•**Diving tours**: Look under "Snorkeling" and "Scuba Diving Tours."
•**Driving**: "Tours" or "Sightseeing Tours."
•**Glider rides**: "Gliders."
•**Helicopter tours**: "Helicopter Charter and Rental Service."
•**Sailing and cruises**: "Boats-Charter."
•**Submarine rides**: In Honolulu, phone Atlantis Submarines Hawaii, 522-1710, for reservations; in Kona, 1-329-6626.

TRADE WINDS

Steady trade winds from the northeast are responsible for Hawaii's balmy weather. Average speed is 11.5 miles an hour. June, July, and August are liable to be a bit more windy about 90 percent of the time. The "trades" usually are lightest in January and February, when "kona" storms sometimes intrude. The kona (south) winds, especially during the winter, tend to bring rain and humid weather.

Tsunami Date	Height	Deaths	Damage
April 1, 1946	55.8 ft	159	$26,000,000
Nov. 4, 1952	20 ft	0	1,000,000
March 9, 1957	52.5 ft	0	5,000,000
May 22, 1960	34.5 ft	61	23,000,000
March 27, 1964	15.7 ft	0	67,590
Nov. 29, 1975	48 ft	2	1,500,000

NOTE: *Honolulu and the Neighbor Islands all have tsunami warning sirens that are tested on the first of each month. Each island's telephone directories have maps showing areas that might be flooded.*

TSUNAMIS

The word "tsunami" comes to science from the Japanese who have had centuries of experience with these seismic "tidal waves." Serious tsunamis have hit Hawaii several times in the past century, normally as a consequence of earthquakes thousands of miles from our shore. The six most destructive were: *see table above.*

UKULELE

'Jumping Flea'

Ubiquitous in Hawaiian music and as symbolic of Hawaii as the lei, the *ukulele*'s literal meaning is "jumping flea." Introduced by Portuguese immigrants a century ago, it was popularized worldwide when Arthur Godfrey began strumming one on his television show.

VISITOR INDUSTRY

Tourism, the number one industry in Hawaii, attracted approximately 7 million people in 1990. They spent $9.4 billion. More than 90 percent of Hawaii's visitors are impressed with what they find here; 36 percent call it "far superior" and 55 percent say "above average" when asked to compare it with other vacation places. More than half of our west-bound vacationers (from continental U.S. or Europe) are repeat visitors! Their average stay is ten days; travelers heading beyond Hawaii stay five days.

Oahu (Honolulu) is the most popular island, drawing 70 percent. Neighbor island popularity is steadily growing. The last survey showed 42 percent going to Maui, 30 percent to Kauai, and almost 28 percent to the Big Island. For Visitor Information, see Hawaii Visitors Bureau above.

VOLCANOES

The Hawaiian Archipelago stretches almost 1,600 miles across the Pacific Ocean, and all 132 of its islands originated from volcanic action. The long-running lava flow from Kilauea crater on the Big Island (see Geography and Geology for more information) shows that parts of the State are still actively volcanic.

Kilauea erupting

Recent Volcanic Activity in Hawaii

	Duration in days	Volume of Lava in thousands of cubic yds.
Haleakala, Maui	N/A	N/A
last active in 1790		
Hualalai, Hawaii		
last active in 1800-1801	N/A	N/A
Kilauea, Hawaii		
February 22, 1969	6	22,000
May 24, 1969	867	242,000
August 14, 1971	<1	12,400
September 24, 1971	5	10,500
February 4, 1972	455	163,800
May 5, 1973	<1	1,600
November 10, 1973	30	3,700
December 12, 1973	203	39,300
July 19, 1974	3	9,000
September 19, 1974	<1	14,000
December 31, 1974	<1	19,600
November 29, 1975	<1	300
September 13, 1977	18	45,000
November 16, 1979	1	800
April 30, 1982	<1	260
September 25, 1982	<1	3,900
January 3, 1983 to present	3650 and counting	1,700,000
Mauna Loa, Hawaii		
July 5, 1975	<1	35,000
March 25, 1984	22	230,000

WEATHER

Dress for summer. Normal daily high temperatures range from 81° to 84° Fahrenheit year around. Honolulu is generally warmer, averaging around 84°. Hilo and Lihue are cooler by about three degrees. Nightly lows are 65° to 69°. May to October are the warmer months, August and September being the hottest. Things are cooler between October and April, with January and February the coolest.

Come prepared for lots of sunshine. Hawaii typically has only 100 days a year with 0.01 inches or more of rain. That means the other 265 days are just fine for leaving your umbrella at home.

Relative humidity is usually between 56 and 72 percent. Average ocean temperatures fluctuate between 75° and 80° F.

WILDLIFE

Forty-eight species of birds are counted in the Honolulu area (1990), including seven found nowhere else in the world. Hawaii's unique *nene* goose can be seen at the Honolulu Zoo and the rare Hawaiian monk seal at the Waikiki Aquarium. Deer, wild turkey, feral goats, feral sheep, feral pigs, quail, pheasants, and partridge are found on most islands, and can be hunted with proper licenses.

WIND-SURFING

Honolulu visitors and residents alike line up almost daily to watch daredevil wind-surfers challenge the ocean off the Diamond Head Light-house. On the windward side of Oahu, Kailua

Kailua Bay board-sailors

Bay is well known for its wind-surfing. The steady trade winds on the Neighbor Islands, particularly at Maui's world-famous Hookipa Beach Park, attract appreciative crowds.

Several outfits will do everything for you, from renting the equipment to picking you up and teaching you how to use a sailboard. They are listed in the yellow pages under "Wind-surfing."

ZORI

The throngs wear thongs

Comfort is the bottom line in Hawaii, and it starts with your feet. Shoes, while tolerated, are usually saved for church or office. The preferred footwear is the ubiquitous *zori*, or "flipflop" slipper. The favorite is inexpensive rubber. Pick up a pair and relax.

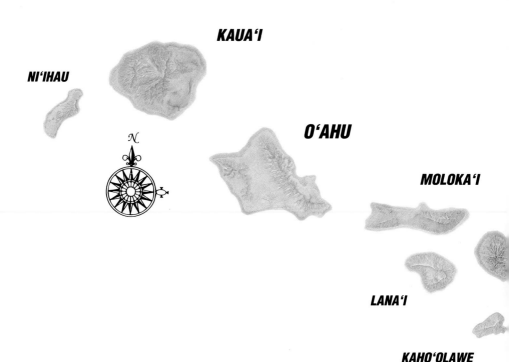

KAUA'I

NI'IHAU

N

O'AHU

MOLOKA'I

LANA'I

KAHO'OLAWE

THE HAWAIIAN ISLANDS

E ach of Hawaii's islands—the Big Island of Hawaii, Kahoolawe, Kauai, Lanai, Maui, Molokai, Niihau, and Oahu—has its own personality. In the chapters that follow, brief introductions, suggested tours, and an alphabetic mini-encyclopedia will familiarize you with each major island, highlighting scenic, cultural, and historical attractions.

The tours assume you'll be staying in one of the major resort areas and will have access to a car.

Feel free to mix and match our tour suggestions with your own ideas, and with other recommendations. And, of course, if you find a beach you never want to leave, just let your travel agent know. Happy traveling!

HAWAII THE ALOHA STATE

••••••••••••••••••••••••••••••••

- Discovered by Polynesian settlers between the 3rd and 7th centuries A.D.; by British Captain James Cook in 1778.

- Admitted to the Union August 21, 1959, as the 50th State.

- Subtropical climate: normal, annual temperature: 77 degrees Fahrenheit at Honolulu International Airport.

- Hawaii is a string of islands (6,423.4 sq. land mi.) in the north central Pacific, about 2,400 miles west of San Francisco.

- Resident population: 1,159,000

  De facto population: 1,300,600 (includes average daily visitors and Hawaii based armed forces and their dependents).

- Population density statewide (1990): 194 people per square mile.

- Major ethnic groups: Caucasians, 23%; Japanese, 21%; mixed race, primarily part-Hawaiian, 35%. Groups include Filipinos, 4%; Chinese,4%; Blacks, 2%; Koreans,1%.

- Hawaii's Economy (1992) Gross State Product: $29.3 billion.

  Visitor expenditures: $9.9 billion.
  Federal defense spending: $3.3 billion.
  Sugar production: $271 million.
  Pineapple production: $225 million.

MAUI

HAWAI'I

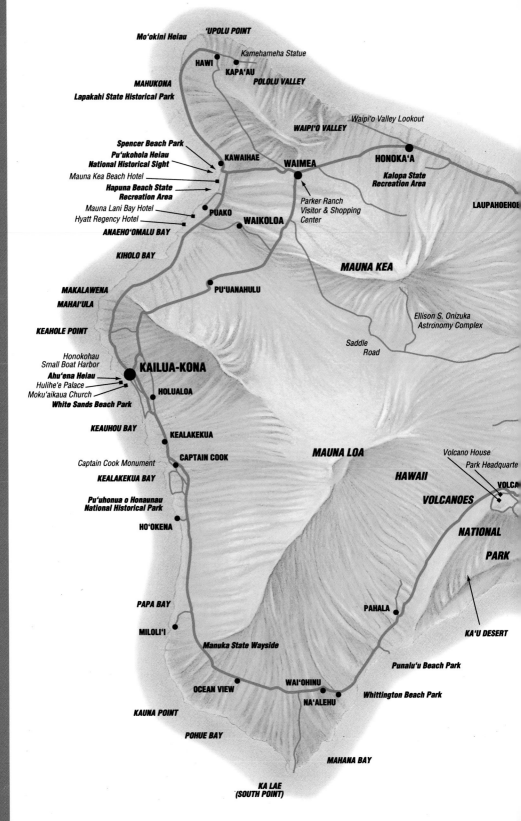

Mo'okini Heiau

'UPOLU POINT

Kamehameha Statue

HAWI

KAPA'AU

POLOLU VALLEY

MAHUKONA

Lapakahi State Historical Park

Waipi'o Valley Lookout

WAIPI'O VALLEY

HONOKA'A

Spencer Beach Park
Pu'ukohola Heiau
National Historical Sight

KAWAIHAE

WAIMEA

Kalopa State
Recreation Area

Mauna Kea Beach Hotel

Hapuna Beach State
Recreation Area

LAUPAHOEHOE

Mauna Lani Bay Hotel
Hyatt Regency Hotel

PUAKO

WAIKOLOA

Parker Ranch
Visitor & Shopping
Center

ANAEHO'OMALU BAY

KIHOLO BAY

MAUNA KEA

MAKALAWENA

MAHAI'ULA

PU'UANAHULU

Ellison S. Onizuka
Astronomy Complex

KEAHOLE POINT

Saddle
Road

Honokohau
Small Boat Harbor

KAILUA-KONA

Ahu'ena Heiau
Hulihe'e Palace
Moku'aikaua Church

HOLUALOA

White Sands Beach Park

KEAUHOU BAY

KEALAKEKUA

MAUNA LOA

Volcano House

Park Headquarte

CAPTAIN COOK

HAWAII

VOLCA

Captain Cook Monument

KEALAKEKUA BAY

VOLCANOES

Pu'uhonua o Honaunau
National Historical Park

NATIONAL

HO'OKENA

PARK

PAPA BAY

PAHALA

KA'U DESERT

MILOLI'I

Manuka State Wayside

Punalu'u Beach Park

OCEAN VIEW

WAI'OHINU

Whittington Beach Park

KAUNA POINT

NA'ALEHU

POHUE BAY

MAHANA BAY

KA LAE
(SOUTH POINT)

ISLAND OF HAWAII

AKAKA FALLS

ONOMEA BAY
RAINBOW FALLS
Lyman Museum
Lili'uokalani Gardens
Leleiwi Beach Park

HILO

na'ewa
Zoo

KEA'AU

MOUNTAIN VIEW

CAPE KUMUKAHI

Lava Tree
State Monument

PAHOA

Isaac Hale Beach Park
POHOIKI

PU'U O'O CRATER

KALAPANA

KAMOAMOA

- The State's largest island, known as the "Big Island."

- Measures 4,028 square miles in land area—almost twice the combined size of the other islands.

- The youngest island in the Hawaiian Islands chain. The Big Island was formed by five volcanoes, two still active.

- Holds the southernmost U. S. point (Ka Lae).

- Second most populous island in the State, with a resident population of 130,500.

- Climate in coastal regions is warm, and semi-tropical. Higher areas: cooler. Mauna Kea summit: temperature range about 31 to 43 degrees. Winter brings frost above the 4,000-foot level and snow above 10,000 feet on Mauna Loa and Mauna Kea.

- Average annual rainfall: 128 inches at Hilo Airport, 10 inches near Kawaihae.

Big Island—Home of Madam Pele

HAWAII:
THE BIG ISLAND

While the State's other islands were formed by single volcanoes or the merging of two, Hawaii, The Big Island, is the work of five major volcanoes. Two—Mauna Loa and Kilauea—are still active. As the youngest of the islands, Hawaii has few beaches or reefs, but it yields to no other in size and grandeur, rising from 18,000 feet deep to soar to nearly 14,000 feet above sea level. The island of Hawaii is twice the size of all the other islands combined.

It was also the home of Hawaii's most famous monarch, the invincible warrior and shrewd statesman, Kamehameha the Great. A Kohala chief who saw Captain Cook slain at Kealakekua Bay in 1779, Kamehameha by the time of his death 40 years later had united the once warring islands into a single peaceful kingdom.

As befits the cradle of the monarchy and the State's only actively volcanic island, Hawaii remains one of the most "Hawaiian" places. Ancient ties to the volcano goddess Pele are still strong, and the tradition of environmental stewardship has made many Big Islanders vigorous opponents of such modern developments as geothermal power plants, manganese nodule refineries and commercial spaceports that others propose for their island.

More benign ventures such as ocean thermal energy conversion (OTEC), aquaculture, coffee, papaya and macadamia nut production, astronomy, and even some resort developments have had a kinder reception by Big Islanders seeking viable economic alternatives to the fading sugar and ranching industries.

Hawaii island is justly renowned for its steamy Hawaii Volcanoes National Park, the emerald ranch lands of Kohala, Kamuela and Honokaa, and the soft rain-pelted beauty of Hilo, the island's "county seat."

The only island with its own desert and with regular annual snowfall, Hawaii boasts of having the southernmost point in the United States (South Point, or Ka Lae) and the nation's rainiest city (Hilo). The 150-year-old Parker Ranch may be America's largest privately owned spread.

The leeward Kona and South Kohala coasts have witnessed phenomenal hotel and condominium development in the past twenty-five years.

The Big Island's flower, Lehua.

TOURING THE BIG ISLAND

Each of the Big Island's districts is as large as any one of the other islands, so touring here takes more time.

1. KAILUA-KONA AND SOUTH KONA

Starting in the busy resort community of Kailua-Kona, stroll along the waterfront and Alii Drive with its shops and restaurants. Explore the restored Ahuena Heiau (temple) of Kamehameha the Great on the grounds of the King Kamehameha Hotel near where the king spent his last years and where he died in 1819; Mokuaikaua Church, Hawaii's most venerable Christian church; and Hulihee Palace, summer home of King Kalakaua. Spend an hour browsing through the art and craft galleries in Holualoa, a couple of miles above Kailua-Kona on Mamalahoa Highway.

About half an hour south, past the resorts and golf courses of Keauhou, the town of Captain Cook is the center of Hawaii's own rich Kona coffee cultivation, the only commercially grown coffee in the United States. Several coffee mills offer tours. Other points of interest include Napoopoo and Kealakekua Bay, where Captain Cook met his death. Today the historic bay is a busy snorkeling spot and for good reason.

A few miles farther south, set on a rocky beach, is the palm-shaded City of Refuge National Park (Pu'uhonua

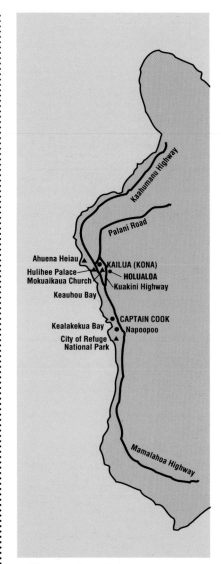

o Honaunau), with its ancient stone walls. Hawaiians fleeing punishment once found protection here. It's a special place for a sunset picnic.

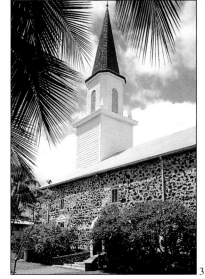

1. Ahu'ena Heiau
2. Kona coffee
3. Moku'aikaua Church
4. City of Refuge at
   Pu'uhonua o Honaunau
5. Cook Monument at Kealakekua Bay

2. KOHALA

Breakfast at one of the grand resorts on the South Kohala coast northwest of Kailua-Kona (the Hilton Waikoloa Village, Mauna Lani Bay Hotel, or Mauna Kea Beach Hotel, for starters). Then stop for a swim at Hapuna Beach, the Big Island's best. Follow the coastline northward to scenic Hawi and Kapaau villages. Along the way, don't miss Puukohala Heiau, Kamehameha's massive war temple, and Lapakahi State Park, a restored 600-year-old Hawaiian fishing village. At Kapaau you'll see the original statue of King Kamehameha.

At the far end of the road is a breathtaking view of Pololu Valley and the Kohala-Hamakua coastline. The 20-minute hike down to the floor of the valley and its black-sand beach is recommended, but swimming here can be dangerous. The trail starts at the very end of the parking area.

Loop back on Route 250 through the green Kohala uplands for awesome views of the entire west coast of the island, then drive into the ranching center at Waimea (or Kamuela), headquarters of the Parker Ranch, the largest privately held ranch in the United States, with Hawaiian *paniolo* cowboys. This charming country town is going steadily upscale, and several restaurants offer excellent dining.

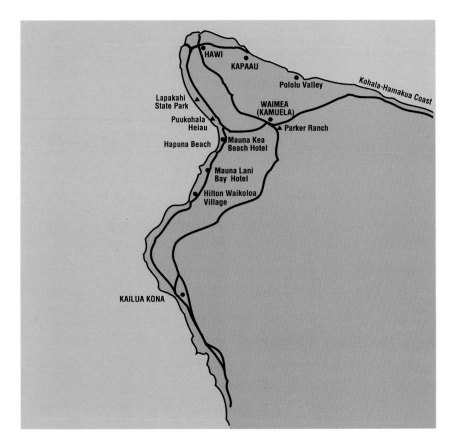

1. *"Paniolo" cowboy*
2. *A Waimea home*
3. *The charming town of Waimea*
4. *Waikoloa, Kohala Coast*

3

1

2

3. HAMAKUA AND HILO

From the old plantation town of Honokaa, drive westward along the coast to the end of the road for a view of scenic Waipio Valley, the biggest valley on the island. This verdant gash in the sea cliffs, with twin waterfalls and a pebbly beach, was once an important population center. Taro is still cultivated here. The narrow road to the valley floor is closed except to four-wheel-drive vehicles, but tours are available.

Back at Honokaa, tour the macadamia nut capital of the world. Along the Hamakua Coast, between deep ravines, sugar cane fields cover every inch of level land. Old mills and plantation towns hang above the sea, but their tranquility reflects the reduced circumstances of "King Sugar."

Laupahoehoe Point, about midway between Honokaa and Hilo, is a beautiful, low-lying peninsula jutting into the pounding surf from the Hamakua cliffs. It hides its tragedy well. A 1946 tsunami wiped out the school that occupied the site, killing 24 teachers and students.

About 15 miles before you reach Hilo, turn off to 420-foot Akaka Falls and its magnificent landscaped gardens.

Verdant (read that rainy) Hilo, low and lush around Hilo Bay beneath the broad majesty of Mauna Kea, is the State's second city and the island's chief harbor. Primary attractions are Rainbow Falls in Wailuku River Park, the 30-acre Liliuokalani Gardens, Hawaii Tropical Botanical Garden, and the Lyman House Memorial Museum. Central Hilo's turn-of-the-century busi-

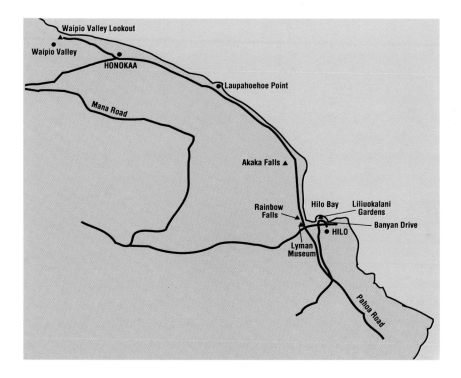

ness district, with covered sidewalks and Pacific port-of-call atmosphere, is being resuscitated with good shops and restaurants. The residential areas above the town are noted for lovely gardens and stout, simple ar-chitecture. Hilo's modest resort area is along Banyan Drive where notables of a generation ago, including Amelia Earhart and FDR, planted impressive rows of shady banyan trees.

1. *Hamakua Coast*
2. *Hawaii's second largest city, Hilo*
3. *Hilo with Mauna Kea in the background*
4. *Laupahoehoe Point*

4. HAWAII VOLCANOES
NATIONAL PARK

From Hilo, a 45-minute drive takes you to Hawaii Volcanoes National Park, where you'll want to spend the whole day. Get an early start!

From the park entrance, head for the visitor center for free road and trail maps, and a filmed explanation of Kilauea volcano's often destructive activity. Then circle Kilauea Caldera, stopping at Volcano House for a magnificent view of the Volcano Observatory, the Thurston Lava Tube, Devastation Trail, the bizarre sulfur pits on the west rim, and Halemaumau Crater where the goddess Pele sometimes shows herself in the smoky clouds. The well-marked hiking trails of all lengths and degrees of difficulty within the park are highly recommended for their never-to-be-forgotten intimacy with Kilauea's primeval landscape. A side trip to the little town of Volcano, an art colony set in a fern forest, is recommended.

It's a full two-hour-plus drive back to your West Hawaii hotel via Hilo, or four hours around South Point. If time and your budget allow, make advance reservations to stay overnight at Volcano House. Then continue the next day after taking advantage of the morning sun to drive to the sea down the spectacular Chain of Craters Road. The road leads to now-isolated Kalapana, where lava has destroyed nearly 200 homes in a slow-motion eruption running since 1983. The shoreline road to the Puna district and its former black-sand beaches is blocked now by lava at Kalapana. Access is possible only from the Hilo side.

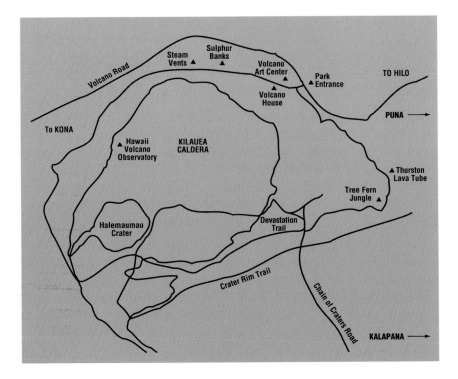

1. *Active Kilauea Volcano*
2. *Ama'u fern, Kilauea*
3. *Thurston Lava Tube*
4. *Volcano National Park*

5. KAU AND SOUTH POINT

From Volcano House, head south past the Kau Desert and Kilauea's Southwest Rift Zone to Punaluu and sleepy Naalehu at the Big Island's southern end. A two-lane road off the main highway soon after you pass Naalehu leads to the southernmost point in the United States. South Point, or Ka Lae, has a green-sand beach as well as remnants of the first Polynesian settlements in Hawaii. Back on the highway, continue northwestward toward Kona and West Hawaii. Consider stopping at little-known Manuka State Park, a 13-acre botanical garden on Route 11.

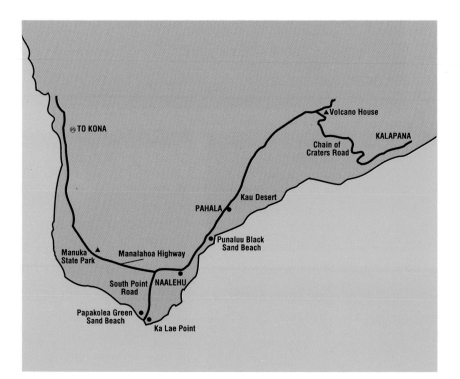

1

4

2

1. *South Point*
2. *Punaluu, a black-sand beach*
3. *South Point*
4. *South Point's green-sand beach*

3

Big Island Facts

AHUENA HEIAU

Restored temple

Formerly covered by a hotel (since demolished), this important temple was restored by the nearby King Kamehameha Hotel with the help of Bishop Museum archaeologists. Kamehameha the Great ruled the Hawaiian Islands from adjoining Kamakahonu ("turtle's eye") after returning from Honolulu in 1812.

AKAKA FALLS STATE PARK

Twice Niagara

Sixty-five-acre Akaka Falls State Park, free to the public, features lush, mostly South American tropical ornamentals and Hawaiian lowland forest plants.

You will find a 442-foot waterfall—more than twice the height of Niagara—heliconia plants, scenic vistas, and trails. Indicated by road signs, the park is on Route 22, 15 miles north of Hilo, near Honomu.

CITY OF REFUGE NATIONAL PARK (PUUHONUA O HONAUNAU)

Fugitives welcomed

Hawaiian custom recognized places of sanctuary for certain types of offenders, such as defeated warriors or violators of the sacred *kapu*, "taboo," system. If they could somehow reach a sanctuary, rites performed by priests would purify these fugitives, who were then free to go back home. Honaunau, an hour's drive south of Kailua-Kona, is one of the largest (181 acres) and is considered the most sacred.

The park is open daily from 6 a.m. to midnight. The visitor center is open daily, 7:30 a.m. to 5:30 p.m. Admission is $1 for adults (over 13). Call 328-2326 or 328-2288 for information, or write P.O. Box 129, Honaunau, Hawaii 96726.

DIVING

The Kona Coast is a diver's heaven. Beginning snorkelers will appreciate sheltered Kahaluu Beach Park, just a few miles south of Kailua-Kona. Snorkelers as well as scuba fans will revel in spectacular Kealakekua Bay, a marine preserve like Hanauma Bay on Oahu, approximately 11 miles farther south. The bay is accessible only by boat. Tour companies can take you there.

FISHING

Tackling big game

The Big Island has great deep-sea fishing. The annual Hawaiian International Billfishing Tournament, the world's leading marlin fishing event, is held there each July or early August. Competing costs big bucks, but watching is cheap. Look under "Fishing Parties" in the yellow pages or ask your hotel tour desk.

GOLF

Designer links

The Big Island has no shortage of championship courses! You can choose from the world-famous Mauna Kea Beach course designed by Arnold Palmer, the Waikoloa Village and Waikoloa Beach courses done by Robert Trent Jones, Jr., the soon-to-be-completed King's Course at Waikoloa by Tom Weiskopf and Jay Morrish, and a dozen others.

HALEMAUMAU CRATER

Once a bubbling lake

Part of Kilauea Volcano at 3,660 feet (1,116 meters) elevation, Halemaumau ("fern house") crater was the most popular tourist attraction in Hawaii from 1823 to 1924, when it contained a bubbling lake of lava. See it when you visit Hawaii Volcanoes National Park.

HAMAKUA COAST

Macnut mecca

As you head northwest out of Hilo along Highway 19, notice the lush green expanse of Hamakua Coast sugar cane. Remember to stop in Honokaa, the "macadamia nut capital." Pause to see fertile Waipio Valley, once the home of Hawaii's kings.

HAWAII TROPICAL BOTANICAL GARDEN

Jungle journey

Private; admission charge; 16 and under free. Open 8:30 a.m. to 5:30 p.m. This lush 25-acre tropical forest (primarily exotics) with trails and waterfalls is approximately seven miles north of Hilo on a four-mile scenic drive near Pepeekeo. Call 964-5233 for information.

HAWAII VOLCANOES NATIONAL PARK

America's newest land

The most visited spot on the Big Island is the State's largest park (207,643 acres). Thirty miles south of Hilo on Route 11, it dwarfs Maui's 27,350-acre Haleakala National Park, the second largest. Open 7:30 a.m. to 5 p.m. The entrance fee is $5 per car. Write Hawaii Volcanoes National Park, P.O. Box 52, Hawaii 96718, or call 967-7311.

HILO

Rustic and rainy

With the only deep water harbor on the Big Island, Hilo is the Hawaii County seat. Its main scenic attractions are Rainbow Falls in Wailuku River Park; the Boiling Pots below the falls in the same river; thirty-acre Liliuokalani Gardens, visible beside the sea as you fly into Hilo; Suisan Fish Market (watch the 7:30 a.m. auction of the night's catch); the Hawaii Tropical Botanical Garden; and the Lyman Mission House and Museum.

HULIHEE PALACE

Royal holidays

A Kailua-Kona landmark, this restored vacation residence of Hawaiian royalty was built in 1837. Hawaiian featherwork, quilts, *tapa*, and royal furniture are on display. Open 9 a.m. to 4 p.m. (closed on major holidays). Admission charge. Located at Alii Drive, Kailua-Kona. Call 329-1877 for information.

IRONMAN TRIATHLON

World-class athletes

Now well into its second decade, this premier endurance event held in Kailua-Kona each October involves swimming 2.4 miles, biking 112 miles, and running 26.2 miles. Its first year, 1978, attracted only 15 entrants. Now carried on ABC's "Wide World of Sports" each year, in 1991 it had 1,379 participants. Triathletes typically train 18 to 25 hours a week for eight months before the Ironman, swimming a weekly average of seven miles, biking 232 miles, and running 48 miles.

JAGGER VOLCANO MUSEUM

If you are interested in volcanoes, visit this institution adjacent to the volcano observatory in Hawaii Volcanoes National Park. You can also browse in the bookstore and take a self-guided tour. Open 8:30 a.m. to 5 p.m. Park entrance fee $5 per car. Call 967-7643 for information.

KAILUA-KONA

Hawaii's party town

This famous community's proper name is simply Kailua, but "Kona" is always added to differentiate it from Honolulu's bedroom community of the same name. The heart of the Kona coast and a main resort area, it's a place for leisurely browsing, incredible diving, snorkeling, or fishing, and just plain relaxing. See Mokuaikaua Church (built in 1823, it's the oldest on the island) and Hulihee Palace while you are in town. Major events here are annual deep-sea fishing tournaments, the October Ironman Triathlon, and the annual Kona Coffee Festival in November. Don't forget Holualoa with its art galleries, just 15 minutes up Mamalahoa Highway.

KALOPA STATE RECREATIONAL AREA

Free. Features an arboretum and a 0.7-mile nature hike in native forests. Near Honokaa, 50 miles north of Hilo, off Route 19.

KAMUELA MUSEUM

Remembering early years

Located at the junction of Routes 19 and 250, on the edge of Waimea town (also called Kamuela), this interesting museum houses ancient Hawaiian tools, antique American and Chinese furniture, and other art objects. Open 8 a.m. to 4 p.m., including holidays. Admission charge for adults is $5.00, children under twelve $2. Write P.O. Box 507, Kamuela, Hawaii 96743 or call 885-4724.

KEALAKEKUA BAY

This large bay, "pathway of the gods" in Hawaiian, lies south of Keauhou on the Kona coast. It is famous as the spot where Captain James Cook, the great seafaring explorer, was slain (see General Information chapter). The bay, a marine preserve, is a favorite of snorkelers and scuba divers. The Captain Cook Monument and Hikiau Heiau are along the shore. Drive south from Kailua-Kona past Keauhou on Queen Kaahumanu Highway (Route 11).

Cook's last stand

KILAUEA VOLCANO

Pele's pyrotechnics

One of the world's most active volcanoes and the central attraction of Hawaii Volcanoes National Park, Kilauea ("spewing") is the legendary home of Pele, the Hawaiian goddess of fire. The eleven-mile Crater Rim Drive circles the volcanic caldera, passing giant Halemaumau Crater, the volcano observatory, steam vents, sulfur banks, and the Thurston Lava Tube. For park hours see Hawaii Volcanoes National Park above.

KING KAMEHAMEHA STATUE, KAPAAU

This statue of Kamehameha the Great, unifier of the Hawaiian Islands, is the original cast by American sculptor Thomas R. Gould. When the ship carrying it to Hawaii caught fire and was beached near Cape Horn, another was cast and shipped to Hawaii in 1883. (The second statue today stands in front of the State judiciary building in Downtown Honolulu.) Later the original was salvaged, repaired, and sent to Kamehameha's North Kohala birth site, where it now stands outside the courthouse.

KING KAMEHAMEHA STATUE, KAPAAU

Shipwreck salvage

KIPUKA PUAULU BIRD PARK

Free admission. 100 acres, two miles west of Volcano House in Hawaii Volcanoes National Park. A self-guided nature trail has labeled trees and many rare native plants and birds. Follow Route 11 to Mauna Loa Strip Road.

KOHALA COAST

From lava to luxury

If you head north from Kailua-Kona along Queen Kaahumanu Highway (Route 19), you will find miles of white-sand beaches, golf fairways, and luxury hotels.

Complementing the Mauna Kea Beach Hotel and the Mauna Lani Bay Hotel, the two original "big name" destinations, are the recently completed Hyatt Regency Waikoloa fantasyland and the renovated Royal Waikoloan, with half a dozen more under construction or on the drawing boards. Ancient Hawaiian petroglyphs are worth looking for farther up the road at Puako. Switching to Route 270 as you continue north, you will pass Puukohala Heiau, a massive stone temple, and Lapakahi State Park. At the far north end is Kapaau, where the original statue of King Kamehameha I stands.

KONA COAST

The Kona ("leeward") Coast is the southwestern side of the Big Island. Kailua-Kona is the largest town and one of its oldest. The area's major offerings are fishing and diving, Kealakekua Bay, Captain Cook's monument, Keauhou Bay, and the City of Refuge National Park at Honaunau. Kona is also the home of the only coffee commercially grown grown in the United States.

The **Kona Historical Society**, in the historic (mid-1800s) Greenwell Store in the town of Captain Cook, is the caretaker of historical maps, photos, and manuscripts of local interest. Open Tuesday through Friday, 9 a.m. to 3 p.m. Free, but donations are welcome. Write P.O. Box 398, Captain Cook, Hawaii 96704 or call 323-3222.

Serene Kailua-Kona bay and town

LAPAKAHI STATE PARK

Popular history

The State's only historical park, Lapakahi State Park on the North Kohala coast is second in popularity only to Volcanoes National Park. This partially restored 600-year-old Hawaiian fishing village shows how Hawaiians lived centuries ago.

The park—open free of charge, Monday through Saturday, 8 a.m. to 4 p.m.—has self-guided tours. Write P. O. Box 100, Kapaau, Hawaii 96755 for information. On the Big Island call 889-5566; on Oahu, 548-7455.

LAVA TREE STATE MONUMENT

Volcanic landscapes

An unusual forest of lava molds and native trees. Free. On Route 132 (off Route 13), near Pahoa, 15 miles south of Hilo.

LILIUOKALANI GARDENS

Shades of Japan

Queen Liliuokalani was Hawaii's last native ruler. This Japanese-style array of ponds, pagodas, and bridges close to Hilo Airport is one of the largest formal oriental gardens outside Japan. Located off Banyan Drive, on Hilo Bay.

LYMAN MISSION HOUSE AND MUSEUM

Facts and artifacts

Built in 1839, Lyman House is the oldest frame building in Hilo. Well worth a visit, the museum has added a modern gallery with scientific displays, Hawaiian artifacts and historical exhibits, plus a gift shop. Open Monday through Saturday, 9 a.m. to 5 p.m. (Closed New Year's Day, Fourth of July, Thanksgiving, and Christmas.) Admission charged. 276 Haili Street, Hilo, Hawaii 96720. Call 935-5021 for information.

MANUKA STATE WAYSIDE PARK

Leafy treats

Free admission. This relatively un-known 13-acre park has both native and introduced trees. Forty-one miles south of Kailua-Kona, on Route 11.

MAUNA KEA

The tallest peak in Hawaii at 13,796 feet (4,205 meters), Mauna Kea ("white mountain") is listed (condi-tionally) by the Guinness Book of Records as the tallest mountain in the world. From its sea-floor base at 3,280 fathoms (19,680 feet) in the Hawaiian Trough, it rises a towering total of 33,476 feet!

Telescopes on Mauna Kea have a view of the skies unsurpassed in the Northern Hemisphere. The cold, rar-efied air minimizes the usual distor-tion caused by light and heat. Mauna Kea's nine telescopes scan the skies each night with cameras and comput-ers, recording visible and infrared im-ages of stars and planets. Daytime tem-peratures on Mauna Kea run between 31°F and 42°F. The coldest ever re-corded here (and in the State) was 1.4°F. In winter there is snow skiing! However, the mountain has no bou-tiques, no lifts, and no nightlife. Access is by four-wheel drive or helicopter.

Eyes on the sky

MAUNA LOA

Long, tall saddle

Mauna Loa ("long mountain"), the sec-ond tallest in Hawaii at 13,677 feet (4,169 meters), is one of the State's two active volcanoes (the other is Kilauea). In March 1984, it spewed out 230,000,000 cubic yards of lava in a period of 22 days. Between Mauna Kea and Mauna Loa is the Humuula Saddle. The infamous Saddle Road (Route 200) cuts across the Big Is-land but is considered to be so haz-ardous that driving the road violates most car rental contracts. Going around the shoreline is no problem.

MERRIE MONARCH FESTIVAL

Hilo's popular *hula* competition was named for King David Kalakaua, whose love of parties and pageantry earned his reputation as the "merrie monarch." Overcoming decades of missionary-inspired restrictions, he encouraged a renaissance of the *hula* late in the last century. The three nights of festivities, in which *hula* students, masters, and professional performers compete, typically are held in April at the Edith Kamakaole Auditorium, in Hilo.

PARKER RANCH

Cool cattle country

What is considered to be the largest privately owned ranch in America covers approximately 225,000 acres. Back in 1809 King Kamehameha I granted John Palmer Parker, an American sailor, a two-acre homestead in payment for rounding up wild sheep, goats, and cattle that had been ravaging the area. (The animals, previously unknown in Hawaii, had been brought by Europeans.) Stop at the Parker Ranch Shopping Center in Waimea (Kamuela), where the late Richard Smart, heir to the ranch, started a museum detailing his family's history on the island.

Parker Ranch Visitor Center offers exhibits and videos of Parker Ranch history and operations. Guided tours and demonstrations are available. Located at Parker Ranch Shopping Center, open Monday through Saturday, 10 a.m. to 4 p.m. Van tours offer special rates for Hawaii residents, children, and senior citizens. Call 885-7655 for information.

Parker Ranch Historic Homes. Located on Highway 190 in Kamuela, the homes include the Mana house built by Parker Ranch founder John Parker in the 1840s and the Puu Opelu house and gallery of the late Richard Smart. Open Monday through Saturday, 10 a.m. to 4 p.m. Admission charge. Call 885-7655.

PELE THE VOLCANO GODDESS

The goddess Pele   © Herb Kane

Legend says that when Pele came to Hawaii, she first dug a cave by the beach at Haena, on Kauai island, hoping to set up housekeeping there. Striking water, she tried again nearby with the same result. Disgusted, she traveled from one island to the next, finally finding a suitable dwelling in the Halemaumau firepit on the Big Island, after scaring off Ailaau, the ancient fire god and previous occupant of the Big Island's volcanoes.

PUNALUU BLACK SAND BEACH

Ebony shores

This interesting beach on the Puna shore, south of Hawaii Volcanoes National Park, has famous black sand, created when red-hot lava exploded as it flowed into the sea. Wave action wore down chunks of black lava into grains of sand.

RAINBOW FALLS

Shimmering cascades

Hilo's iridescent cascade took its name from frequent rainbows seen when the sun catches the spray and mist below the falls. It is just past Hilo Hospital, in Wailuku River Park. Follow the signs out Waianuenue Avenue.

THURSTON LAVA TUBE

Magma tunnel

When a river of hot lava cools on the surface, forming a shell, the still molten lava beneath may continue to flow, resulting in a lava tube. Don't miss walking through this easily accessible one in Hawaii Volcanoes National Park.

VOLCANO HOUSE

On the edge of creation

This is another "must" stop in Hawaii Volcanoes National Park. Where else in the world can you dine while looking into a volcano? Make sure to look at the fireplace, which has been burning constantly for nearly a century.

WAILUKU RIVER

Wailuku ("water of destruction") River has the distinction of discharging the greatest average volume of water in the State—185 million gallons a day. The river, the longest on the island, runs 32 miles from the slopes of Mauna Kea to Hilo Bay.

WAIMANU VALLEY

Water wonders

This valley in the Kohala area is famous for its eighteen-mile-long "ditch," christened in 1906 after workmen excavated 44 tunnels to divert the flow of water from the valley's head to irrigate the Hamakua Coast sugar plantations. The tunnels are eight feet wide and seven feet high, the longest nearly a half mile. The ditch culminates in an 850-foot manmade waterfall.

WAIPIO VALLEY

Sheer beauty

The largest valley on the Big Island, Waipio is a mile wide at its mouth on the beach and extends back six miles into the Kohala mountains. Cascading waterfalls accent its lush, green beauty. Once heavily populated, few people have lived there since a disastrous tsunami in 1946 swept virtually everything out to sea. At the end of Highway 24 on the Honokaa coast, off Highway 19, the valley can be entered in a four-wheel-drive vehicle (a shuttle is usually available) or on foot. But you might consider a commercial ground tour or seeing it by helicopter.

WAIMEA

Upcountry Hawaii

The Waimea ("reddish water") district is the Big Island equivalent of Maui's "Upcountry." It is primarily ranchland and famous for the Parker Ranch, said to be the largest privately owned ranch in the United States, but is steadily going upscale. The town of Waimea is also called Kamuela (Hawaiian for "Samuel"). See Parker Ranch above.

Paniolo Country

ISLAND OF KAHOOLAWE

• 44.6 square miles (uninhabited); formerly used as a bombing practice range by the Navy and Marine Corps.

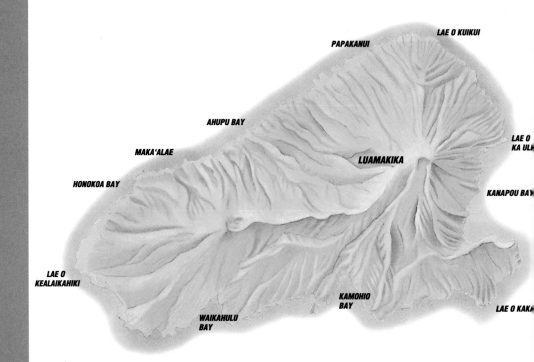

LAE O KUIKUI

PAPAKANUI

AHUPU BAY

MAKA'ALAE

LUAMAKIKA

LAE O KA ULU

HONOKOA BAY

KANAPOU BAY

LAE O KEALAIKAHIKI

KAMOHIO BAY

LAE O KAKA

WAIKAHULU BAY

KAHOOLAWE

Sheltered by the vast bulk of nearby Haleakala from Hawaii's moisture-laden northeast trade winds, low-lying Kahoolawe is now barren red "hard pan," impenetrable to rain or roots. Kahoolawe translates as "the carrying away," and the island has indeed been carried away in a 200-year plume of fine red dust.

Inhabited only intermittently in ancient times by fishermen and gatherers of obsidian crystals (for spear points), Kahoolawe enjoyed a brief commercial career in the 1930s as an offshore annex to Maui's Haleakala and Ulupalakua ranches. But with the approach of World War II, civilian access was curtailed and since 1940 the island has absorbed millions of rounds of U.S. and Allied naval and aircraft gunfire.

Molokai Hawaiians in 1977 "occupied" Kahoolawe for several days, eluding military searchers and bringing the bombardment to a temporary halt. A decade of litigation, media warfare, and negotiation followed between a Hawaiian people's advocacy group and a surprisingly tolerant U.S. Navy. It took a hotly contested U.S. Senate race to get top-level action.

Looking toward the day when the island will revert to State ownership and nonmilitary use, Navy sharpshooters have been destroying the island's destructive goats. Joint military-civilian forestry teams have planted thousands of dry-land trees in hopes of once again attracting rainfall to the barren slopes.

One long-range vision sees Kahoolawe as an undeveloped wilderness park, the only island area preserved in anything like its natural state. Meanwhile, Kahoolawe is a magnet for fishermen and scuba divers who harvest the plentiful game fish off its shores. Kahoolawe itself is off limits to all but military personnel most of the year.

While it has rarely been prominent commercially, Kahoolawe often has been useful. Pre-Cook navigators supposedly used island landmarks as guides for starting the long voyage back to Tahiti, and nineteenth century opium runners found the deserted island handy. Their legacy today is a sandy "Smugglers' Cove."

Hina hina, grown on Kahoolawe

1. *No longer a bombing practice range*
2. *Former smugglers haven*

Haleakala rises in the distance

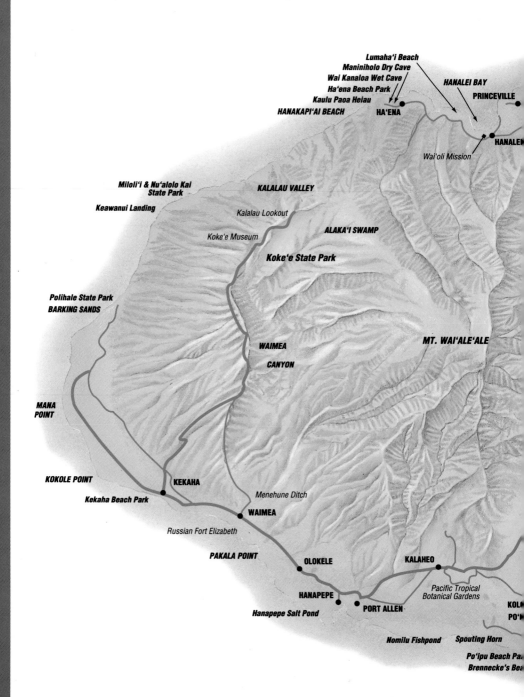

Lumaha'i Beach
Maniniholo Dry Cave
Wai Kanaloa Wet Cave
Ha'ena Beach Park
Kaulu Paoa Heiau
HANAKAPI'AI BEACH

HANALEI BAY

PRINCEVILLE

HA'ENA

HANALE

Wai'oli Mission

Miloli'i & Nu'alolo Kai
State Park

Keawanui Landing

KALALAU VALLEY

Kalalau Lookout

Koke'e Museum

ALAKA'I SWAMP

Koke'e State Park

Polihale State Park
BARKING SANDS

WAIMEA

CANYON

MT. WAI'ALE'ALE

MANA
POINT

KOKOLE POINT

Kekaha Beach Park

KEKAHA

Menehune Ditch

WAIMEA

Russian Fort Elizabeth

PAKALA POINT

OLOKELE

KALAHEO

Pacific Tropical
Botanical Gardens

KOL

HANAPEPE

PO'

Hanapepe Salt Pond

PORT ALLEN

Nomilu Fishpond

Spouting Horn

Po'ipu Beach Pa

Brennecke's Bea

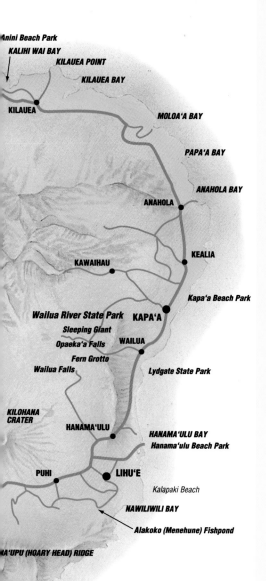

Anini Beach Park
KALIHI WAI BAY
KILAUEA POINT
KILAUEA BAY
KILAUEA
MOLOA'A BAY
PAPA'A BAY
ANAHOLA BAY
ANAHOLA
KEALIA
KAWAIHAU
Kapa'a Beach Park
Wailua River State Park   **KAPA'A**
Sleeping Giant
Opaeka'a Falls   **WAILUA**
Fern Grotto
Wailua Falls   **Lydgate State Park**
KILOHANA CRATER
HANAMA'ULU
HANAMA'ULU BAY
Hanama'ulu Beach Park
PUHI   **LIHU'E**
Kalapaki Beach
NAWILIWILI BAY
Alakoko (Menehune) Fishpond
HA'UPU (HOARY HEAD) RIDGE

ISLAND OF KAUAI

• Known as "the Garden Island."

• Smallest in size of the four major islands: 552.3 sq. miles land area.

• Geologically, Kauai is the oldest of Hawaii's major islands, site of the first Hawaii landing by Captain James Cook in 1778. Many movies with South Seas and Asian settings have been shot at the beaches and valleys of Kauai.

• Least populous of the four major island: 52,000.

• Average temperatures near the coast: 71 degrees F. in January-February, 79 degrees F. in August-September. Cooler in mountain areas such as Kokee.

• The summit of Waialeale is the wettest spot in the United States with an average rainfall of 444 inches per year. At the Poipu Beach resort area on the southern coast, rainfall averages only 35 inches per year.

• Two renowned sightseeing destinations: Hanalei Bay, where "South Pacific" was filmed; and Waimea Canyon, the "Grand Canyon of the Pacific."

Enjoying the Na Pali Coast

Once a "high island" like Maui and Hawaii, Kauai has eroded over the eons into broad valleys, windswept escarpments, and low, steep mountains. As the most northerly of Hawaii's eight main islands, Kauai is the first to feel the rainbearing northeast trade winds that prevail at this latitude most of the year.

Although Kauai is by far Hawaii's greenest island, it also has a "dry side" whose most prominent feature is the remarkable Waimea Canyon. Despite this colorful fissure, however, Kauai's most enduring image is of densely forested mountains descending steeply from the clouds to verdant valleys.

Since ancient times, the Garden Island has been known for its independence. Along with Niihau, its small neighbor to leeward, Kauai has enjoyed an out-of-sight, out-of-mind relationship to the rest of the archipelago, from which it is rarely visible. The broad and often stormy channel separating Kauai from Oahu has helped to protect it, twice rebuffing invasion forces of Kamehameha the Great poised on Oahu. Of all the islands, only Kauai and Niihau were never physically overrun by Kamehameha, who finally incorporated them in his kingdom by negotiation.

Kauai is unique in other respects as well.

It is the only island in the State with a navigable river and its own "grand canyon." Its Mount Waialeale is the wettest spot in the nation. And Kauai is the home of the legendary pre-Polynesian race of fishpond builders, the beloved Menehune.

Until recently, Kauai, alone among the major islands, was able to forestall the rapid resort and commercial boom that has transformed Oahu, Maui and the Big Island since Statehood. This "slow growth" consensus was a casualty of Hurricane Iwa that wrecked parts of the island in 1982. Nevertheless, Kauai's reluctance to embrace pell-mell development has given it special standing with discriminating visitors.

Residents and the more than one million visitors each year are largely confined to a coastal strip that stretches from Barking Sands on the dry west side to Kee Beach in lush Haena. Completing the circle between the two road ends is a footpath from Haena along the majestic Na Pali Coast as far as Kalalau Valley. From that point to Barking Sands, transit is only by boat.

From the dry plains of the west side, a great expanse of sugar cane blankets the island all the way to Anahola on the east. Near Kekaha, a second road winds upwards along one rim

Kauai's flower—the mokihana

of Waimea Canyon to Kokee State Park and the fabulous Kalalau Lookout. Lihue, the commercial center of Kauai, sits on a plateau above Nawiliwili Harbor, the island's principal port. Kauai's main airport, largest shopping center and county seat are in Lihue.

On Kauai's south side, a world-class resort community has developed at Poipu. Past Lihue along the coastal highway, the rapidly growing communities of Wailua and Kapaa seem to be merging into one large resort town. Lush green Haena, Hanalei and Princeville at the northern end of the

island have managed to maintain a rural atmosphere.

Kauai also has fostered innovative ventures in agriculture and aquaculture, productive sugar and pineapple plantations, and a thriving arts community. The opening of an ambitious Westin resort near Lihue, the county seat, in the mid-1980s restored tourism to its premier economic position, but the island remains wary lest it become overcrowded.

O Kauai nui moku lehua, aina nui makekau, says an old proverb. "Great Kauai, island of warriors and land of men ever on the defense."

Princeville view of Hanalei

Kauai is essentially round and compact with a volcanic peak at its center. Although some visitors "do" the island in a single day, don't fail to take extra time for golf, hiking, water sports, relaxing or whatever appeals to you. If you fall in love with a spot and decide to enjoy it a while longer, you won't be the first to do so.

1. NORTH AND EAST KAUAI

Begin at Lihue, the Kauai county seat and the island's largest town. Kauai Museum on Rice Street will help orient you. Nawiliwili Harbor is a quintessential South Pacific port; at the other extreme, close by at Kalapaki Beach is the opulent Westin Kauai Hotel with a huge swimming pool and monumental architecture.

North of Lihue, Kuhio Highway passes Wailua, from where small tour boats take visitors to the Fern Grotto and Opaekaa Falls. Beyond Kapaa and Anahola towns, Kilauea Point lighthouse, surrounded by a federal sea bird sanctuary, is a spectacular and educational spot. (Kilauea town has a wonderful general store, bakery and restaurant.) Princeville, a golf-oriented resort community set on cliffs above the sea, is followed by historic Hanalei Valley and Bay, where many of Hollywood's most enduring "South Pacific" images have been filmed.

At the far end of the road are Haena and Kee Beach. On the hillside is a

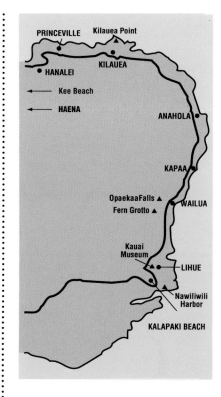

series of stone terraces where, legend says, the goddess Pele danced for the high chief Lohiau in an event famous in Hawaiian mythology. Kee Beach is another of Hawaii's fabulous end-of-the-road beauty spots, a soul-stirring place for an al fresco sunset dinner.

Beyond Kee Beach is the awe-inspiring Na Pali Coast, a stretch of waterfalls, cliffs, tropical forests, and valleys accessible only to hikers and boaters. A helicopter tour from Lihue gives a good view of the coastline. Boat tours operate during summer.

1. Fern Grotto
2. Haena Point
3. The town of Kapaa

1. Kalalau lookout
2. Kokee-Kalalau lookout
3. Pacific Tropical Botanical Gardens

2. SOUTH AND WEST KAUAI

Driving southwest out of Lihue on Kaumualii Highway, turn left into the famous Tree Tunnel on Maluhia Road to the old plantation town of Koloa. Recently restored, Koloa now offers interesting shops, an excellent bar (Koloa Broiler) and several restaurants. Ten minutes further south is Poipu, Kauai's most popular resort area, with fine beaches and sunny weather. West of Koloa (ask for road directions) is the National Tropical Botanical Gardens in Lawai Valley. The adjoining formal gardens of the old Allerton estate at Lawai Kai were laid out by Queen Emma in the 1870s. Reservations are required for the three-hour tour of this outstanding botanical collection.

Further west are Kalaheo, Hanapepe, and Waimea. Out to sea is low-lying Niihau, the "Forbidden Island," privately owned by the Robinson family of Kauai. Good stops in the vicinity are the Hanapepe Salt Ponds, the remains of Fort Elizabeth, now a historical site, the nearby monu-

ment at Waimea Bay marking Captain Cook's 1778 first landing in Hawaii, and the Menehune Ditch.

Waimea Canyon Road leads you up the "Grand Canyon of the Pacific," more than 3,600 feet deep, 10 miles long, and a mile wide. Near the top is Kokee State Park, a 4,345-acre wildlife and plant preserve with a small restaurant, cabins and campsites. At the end of the road and well worth the extra drive is spectacular Kalalau Lookout, high above Kalalau Valley and the Na Pali Coast.

Back at the foot of the Waimea Canyon Road heading west, the Kaumualii Highway passes the plantation town of Kekaha, practically untouched by tourism or fast-food chains. Its beach is broad and flat. At the far end of a rough but passable road are the Barking Sands, the Pacific Missile Range, and Polihale Beach. This beach, set against the towering western Na Pali Coast cliffs, is broad and vast, with powerful waves and dangerous currents. But it has an awesome, end-of-the-earth feeling. (And it's a great sunset-picnic spot.)

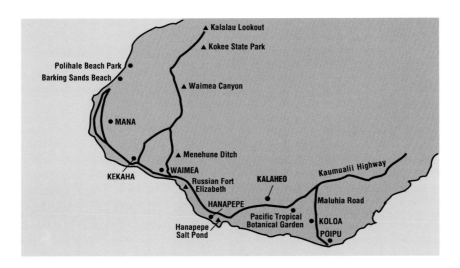

83

KAUAI FACTS

ALAKOKO FISHPOND

Made by Menehune

This "Menehune Fishpond" is enclosed by a 900-foot pre-western-era dam exceptional for its size and engineering. Holes in its thick walls permit tidal circulation but are small enough to prevent fish from escaping. According to legend, *Menehune* (see below) built the fishpond overnight. Still used for raising mullet, Alakoko Pond is in Niumalu, south of Lihue and close to Nawiliwili Harbor.

ALLERTON GARDENS

See National Tropical Botanical Garden.

BARKING SANDS

See Pacific Missile Range.

BLOWHOLE

Like the Halona Blowhole outside Honolulu, this spouts sea water when waves force air through it. The noisy moaning you hear—attributed to

Lehu, a legendary lizard stuck in the hole—is also caused by wave action. South of Lihue on Route 50 and Route 520 through the Tree Tunnel toward Poipu, turn down Lawai Road instead of Poipu Road. You'll find the Spouting Horn near the end of Lawai Road.

'The Spouting Horn'

FERN GROTTO

Romantic favorite

Take a boat trip up the Wailua River to this most romantic place. An open cave filled with thousands of ferns, the grotto is a favorite for island weddings. The small-boat tours out of Wailua Marina take approximately 90 minutes. Departures every 30 minutes, 9a.m. to 4p.m. Call Waialeale Tours at 822-4908 for information.

FORT ELIZABETH STATE PARK

Czarist foothold

Gearg Anton Scheffer, an agent of the Russian American Company, came in the early 1800s to salvage the cargo of a wrecked Russian ship. Under a secret understanding with Kaumualii, then king of Kauai, Scheffer thought he could conquer the rest of the islands. A Russian-style star-shaped fort was constructed near the mouth of Waimea River in 1816. The bid to conquer the islands failed, but the fort remains. The most-visited attraction on Kauai, it is on the southwest shore, just outside Waimea.

HAENA AND NA PALI COAST STATE PARKS

A spectrum of scenery

These adjoining parks, 62 and 6,175 acres respectively, encompass sea-level sites, mountains, dry and wet vegetation, the famous Kalalau Trail along the Na Pali Coast, introduced and native vegetation, a spectacular coastline, and sheer cliffs.

HAENA DRY CAVE (MANINIHOLO)

Lava tube opening

Haena, "red hot," is the site of both dry (Maniniholo) and wet (Waikanaloa and Waikapalae) caves. Off Kuhio Highway (Route 56), past Hanalei and near the end of the road.

HANALEI BAY AND VALLEY

Hanalei ("crescent" in Hawaiian) Bay is the largest on Kauai, the scene of yacht racing during the summer and world-class surfing in winter. The valley, the rice-growing center of Hawaii back in the 1850s, is now famous for its *taro*, producing over 50 percent of Hawaii's crop. The lower 900 acres of this lush valley is a U.S. Fish and Wildlife Service preserve. Be sure to stop at the Hanalei Valley lookout. Located on the island's north side, along Kuhio Highway (Route 56) past Princeville. (photo on next page).

Cinematic backup

HANAPEPE SALT POND BEACH PARK

Old-style solitude

Hanapepe—"crushed bay" (due to landslides)—is a quiet, old-style-Hawaii rural town on the south shore past Kalaheo but before Waimea. At Salt Pond Beach Park just outside of town, local families during the summer still gather the heavy, brownish salt crystals evaporated by the sun from brackish water in these ancient salt pans, just as early Hawaiians did. On Kaumualii Highway (Route 50), out of Lihue.

KALALAU VALLEY LOOKOUT

For a spectacular spot overlooking the largest valley on the Na Pali Coast and one of the best "postcard views" on the island, drive up Waimea Canyon Road (Route 55) past Kokee State Park to the top. Kalalau Valley is considered inaccessible except by helicopter or boat, but adventurous souls have made it down the sheer cliffs. Others hike in over the rugged trail from Haena. Most recommend just admiring this beautiful valley from the lookout. Located out of Waimea on the southern side of the island.

Picture postcard perfect

KAUAI MUSEUM

Hawaiian on display

An art and history museum in Lihue with a Hawaiian collection, a library, photos, tours, and classes. Open Monday through Friday, 9 a.m. to 4:30 p.m.; Saturday 9 a.m. to 1 p.m. Closed major holidays. Adults $3, children up to 17 free when accompanied by an adult. 4428 Rice Street, Lihue. Call 245-6931.

KILAUEA LIGHTHOUSE

Best known for birds

This 52-foot beacon poised two hundred feet above the Pacific on the tip of the Kilauea peninsula no longer flashes all night to guide ships from the Orient past Kauai and on to Oahu. Radio and radar have taken over. When it was built in 1913, its clamshell lens was the largest of its type ever made. Kilauea now is best known for its bird life. Although the lighthouse itself is closed, there is a small park with a visitor center, a gift shop, and restrooms. Open 10 a.m. to 4 p.m., Monday through Friday. Located just outside the town of Kilauea on the north side of Kauai, along Kuhio Highway (Route 56).

KOKEE STATE PARK AND MUSEUM

Up the Waimea Canyon Road from Kauai's southwestern shore, Kokee ("to bend the wind") is a 4,345-acre wildlife and plant preserve with picnic area, State-owned rental cabins, campground, and 45 miles of hiking trails in crisp, cool air. Native rain forest and introduced trees fill the park. On Nualolo-Awapuhi Trail, trees are labeled and an explanatory booklet is available. A lodge and museum provide food and natural history exhibits. Four miles further up through lush tropical rain forest is Kalalau Lookout (see above).

Head up Kokee Road (Route 550) out of Kekaha, or Waimea Canyon Road from Waimea.

Crisp hikes and camping

LIHUE

First stop and shop

Lihue is the county seat and the commercial center of the island. See the Kauai Museum on Rice Street and Grove Farm Homestead. Close by are Alakoko ("Menehune") Fishpond and Nawiliwili Harbor. All flights in and out of Kauai are through Lihue Airport.

LUMAHAI BEACH

Silver screen scenery

Although Kauai is famous for its magnificent beaches, Lumahai is perhaps the most photographed. One look will tell you where much of *South Pacific* was filmed. Lumahai is on Kuhio Highway (Route 56) two miles past Hanalei town toward Haena, on the northern side of the island.

MENEHUNE

Island sprites

Woven into the folklore of Hawaii, the *Menehune* were thought to be a race of tiny, very industrious people who lived here long before the Polynesians came. With magical powers similar to leprechauns, they were able to perform prodigious labor. Few saw them because of their preference for working at night, abandoning anything not completed by sunrise.

Archaeologists who have studied the Menehune Ditch in Waimea, the remains of what was once a great aquaduct, say it contains fitted stonework found nowhere else in Hawaii. Alakoko Fishpond just outside Lihue is attributed to the *Menehune* who, according to legend, built the 900-foot dam overnight.

MENEHUNE FISHPOND

See Alakoko Fishpond above.

NA PALI COAST

You have not really experienced Kauai until you have hiked Na Pali, "the cliffs," an expanse of waterfalls, cliffs, and tropical forests lush with fruits and flowers. The rough and exhausting 11-mile Na Pali Trail stretches from Kee Beach at the end of Kuhio Highway in Haena to Kalalau Valley, and is basically the route used by Hawaiians of old.

The first part of the hike into Hanakapiai Valley is pleasant and takes about an hour. The rest is over cliffs and rocks, and sometimes through mud. Go past the end of the road at Kee Beach to find the trail. Sign the logbook at the beginning of the trail.

The ultimate trek

NAWILIWILI HARBOR

Kauai port of call

Named for a Hawaiian tree bearing small red seeds, this 40-foot-deep harbor is the island's best port with 1,216 linear feet of pier. It is just south of Lihue.

PACIFIC MISSILE RANGE AND BARKING SANDS

Naval war game site

Past Mana, almost at the western end of Route 50, this facility has been the staging area for underwater war games as well as a back-up for the Kokee missile tracking station. A nearby half-mile-long 60-foot-high sand dune is so dry that the sand "barks" when you slide down it.

NATIONAL TROPICAL BOTANICAL GARDEN

Flora galore

Private (arranged tours only), $15 charge per person. Beautiful mature native and introduced trees, heliconias, and other flora abound in this 186-acre garden. Allerton Gardens, a separate, private 100-acre estate adjacent to the National Tropical Botanical Garden, will someday become part of it. Take Route 50 southwest from Lihue, turn left onto Highway 530 at the Lawai cut-off, then right on Hailima Road. Call 332-7361

POIPU BEACH

In Hawaiian, Poipu means "crashing" (as waves). The beach was a sunny haven for ancient Hawaiian chiefs and today is a popular resort destination with first-class hotels, the championship Kiahuna Plantation Golf Course, tennis courts, and one of the best water-sport locations. Wind-surfing, body-surfing, scuba diving, snorkeling, fishing, and sailing are popular along Poipu's more than two miles of sparkling white beaches. (photo on next page).

Poipu Beach

PRINCEVILLE

Planned playground

Named for Kamehameha IV's son who tragically died at the age of four, Princeville is a planned community and major resort development on the north shore of Kauai. Past Kilauea on Highway 56, just before Hanalei Bay, it features a championship golf course, Princeville Shopping Center, luxury accommodations, single-family dwellings, town-houses, and an airport. As you leave, drive to Hanalei Valley Lookout for a great picture!

RUSSIAN FORT STATE HISTORICAL PARK

See Fort Elizabeth State Park

SALT PONDS

See Hanapepe Salt Pond Beach Park.

SLEEPING GIANT

A mountain ridge outside Wailua on Kauai's east side resembles a slumbering giant. Off Kuhio Highway (Route 56), north of Lihue.

SPOUTING HORN

See Blowhole.

TREE TUNNEL

Eucalyptus envelope

This beautiful archway of eucalyptus trees envelop you along the way from Lihue to Poipu. Turn left on to Maluhia Road (Route 520) toward Poipu.

MOUNT WAIALEALE

Kawaikini Peak atop Mount Waialeale ("overflowing water") is the tallest point on Kauai at 5,243 feet (1,598 meters). Mount Waialeale itself measures 5,148 feet (1,569 meters) and is said to be the wettest spot in the world. Average annual rainfall is 444 inches, but an amazing 666 inches was recorded in 1982.

WAILUA RIVER AND FALLS

Famous for Fantasy Island

Wailua ("two waters") Falls was shown at the opening of each episode of *Fantasy Island*. Following a heavy rain, two main streams cascade down an 80-foot drop. The Wailua River is the only navigable stream in Hawaii. From Wailua Marina at the mouth, a boat tour will take you upriver to the Fern Grotto (see separate listing) and the falls.

WAIMEA BAY, CANYON AND STATE PARK

Cook's first tour

Captain Cook stepped ashore for the first time in Hawaii at Waimea ("reddish water") Bay on his third Pacific voyage in 1778. The abortive Russian Fort Elizabeth, overlooking the mouth of Waimea River, is close by.

Be sure to see 36-hundred-foot-deep Waimea Canyon, the Grand Canyon of the Pacific! Go up Kokee Road (Highway 55), or Waimea Canyon Drive. At the end of the road is Kalalau Lookout. The 1,866-acre public **Waimea Canyon State Park** has native and introduced forests, spectacular mountain scenery, and hiking trails. Thirty miles from Lihue. Take Route 50 west and turn off at Waimea on Route 550.

WET CAVES

Eerie water-filled Waikapalae and Waikanaloa caves are where the chiefs are said to have gathered in ancient times. Legend has it that Pele, the volcano goddess, dug these caves herself. See Haena Dry Cave (Maniniholu) above.

ISLAND OF LANAI

- Known as the "Pineapple Isle."
- 140.6 square miles.
- Major industries: tourism with two new luxury resort hotels now open, and pineapple being phased out.
- Population: 2,400

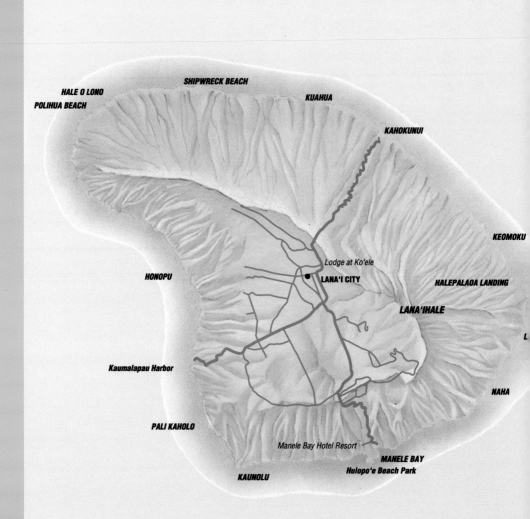

SHIPWRECK BEACH

HALE O LONO

POLIHUA BEACH

KUAHUA

KAHOKUNUI

KEOMOKU

Lodge at Ko'ele

HONOPU

● **LANA'I CITY**

HALEPALAOA LANDING

LANA'IHALE

L

Kaumalapau Harbor

NAHA

PALI KAHOLO

Manele Bay Hotel Resort

MANELE BAY

KAUNOLU

Hulopo'e Beach Park

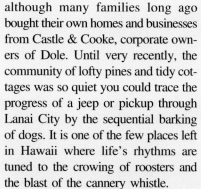

One of the two "dry" islands lying in the rain shadow of Maui's immense Haleakala (uninhabited Kahoolawe is the other), Lanai attracted few settlements in ancient times. Wary of the *uhane* (ghosts) and *akua* (evil beings) which dwelt there, sensible Hawaiians avoided arid Lanai for cooler, moister Maui, Molokai and Oahu.

Pineapple planter James Dole laid the foundation for today's Lanai when he plowed his first pineapple field at Wahiawa, outside Honolulu, in 1901 and founded Hawaii's first successful canning operation. Subsequently, his Dole Corporation purchased 98 percent of Lanai island from the Territorial government. (The remaining two percent is in pie-shape ahupuaa land divisions owned by long-time Hawaiian families.)

Thousands of Norfolk Island and Cook pines were planted to draw moisture from the clouds to supplement the island's limited fresh-water supply. This novel and effective practice has assured a reliable water supply for the State's largest pineapple plantation.

With a population of 2,400, largely descendants of Filipino, Portuguese and Japanese immigrant workers, Lanai City, the lone community, remains the State's foremost "company town,"

although many families long ago bought their own homes and businesses from Castle & Cooke, corporate owners of Dole. Until very recently, the community of lofty pines and tidy cottages was so quiet you could trace the progress of a jeep or pickup through Lanai City by the sequential barking of dogs. It is one of the few places left in Hawaii where life's rhythms are tuned to the crowing of roosters and the blast of the cannery whistle.

As the comparative cost of growing pineapples in Lanai has risen, Castle & Cooke has moved to diversify Lanai's economy. Two world-class resorts were completed in the late 1980s, one at Koele in the upland and the other at Manele Bay. Others are planned for the as-yet-inaccessible eastern beaches. Development is likely to be controlled by the fresh-water supply, the extent of which remains a topic of heated debate.

Like their neighbors across the channel on Molokai, Lanai folks are known for their hunting and fishing skills, their self-sufficiency, their generosity, and their love of family and community. The island is famed for its forested uplands, empty wind-swept beaches and the stark sea cliffs along the western shore, at the foot of which are some of Hawaii's best fishing and diving.

Lanai flower, kaunaoa

LANAI FACTS

DIVING

Lanai's finest

Try Hulopoe Bay's white-sand beach for excellent swimming and diving. Make your arrangements at the hotel.

GOLF

The only place to swing a club at present (1990) is the nine-hole Cavendish golf course. But two 18-hole courses are in the plans. For now, the island's handful of regular golfers welcome guests.

HIKING

Lanaihale, the ridgeline above Lanai City and the greatest elevation on the island, offers scenic hiking, as does the Munro Trail, named for naturalist George C. Munro, who managed Lanai Ranch in 1910. He planted many of the Norfolk Island pines that have become the island's hallmark.

LANAI CITY

Municipal misnomer

The community's two main streets, separated by a central grassy park, are lined with small stores. S. T. Property and Dahang's Bakery are favorites for lunch and breakfast. Everything else shuts down for an hour or so at noon, a plantation tradition that has refused to die. Most stores close at 5:30 p.m.

SIGHTSEEING

The Pinnacles

A four-wheel-drive jeep is best for seeing Lanai. The three brief main roads will not get you very far. Four-wheeling vehicles are in demand during the hunting season and the rental stock is limited, so car reservations should be made by phone well in advance. There are few road signs outside Lanai City. Get directions and advice before going exploring.

Koele Lodge

Pu'u Pehe

Isolated areas such as Kaunolu Bay and an ancient Hawaiian village site on the south side are worthwhile destinations. To the northeast are Shipwreck Beach, deserted Keomuku village, and the remnants of Kahea Heiau.

Be sure to see the "Garden of the Gods," an eerie geologic curiosity whose randomly strewn boulders seem to have been dropped from the sky.

Luahiwa Petroglyphs

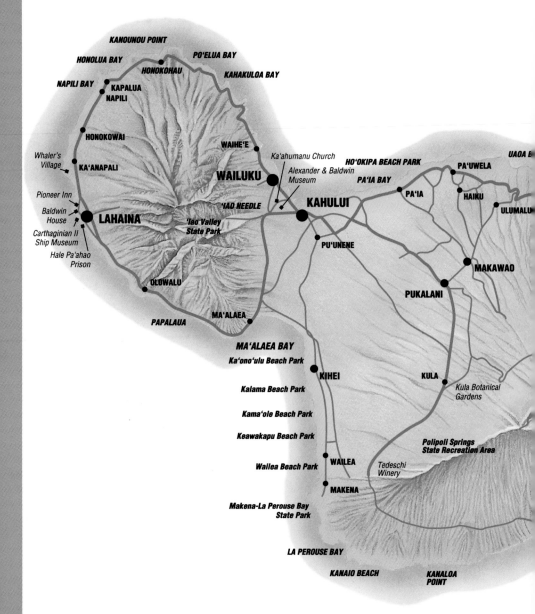

KANOUNOU POINT

HONOLUA BAY
PO'ELUA BAY
HONOKOHAU
KAHAKULOA BAY
NAPILI BAY
KAPALUA
NAPILI

HONOKOWAI
WAIHE'E
Ka'ahumanu Church
HO'OKIPA BEACH PARK
UAOA B
Whaler's
Village
KA'ANAPALI
Alexander & Baldwin
Museum
PA'UWELA
WAILUKU
PA'IA BAY
Pioneer Inn
KAHULUI
PA'IA
HAIKU
Baldwin
House
'IAO NEEDLE
ULUMALU
LAHAINA
'Iao Valley
State Park
Carthaginian II
Ship Museum
Hale Pa'ahao
Prison
PU'UNENE
MAKAWAO
OLOWALU
PUKALANI
MA'ALAEA
PAPALAUA

MA'ALAEA BAY
Ka'ono'ulu Beach Park
KIHEI
KULA
Kalama Beach Park
Kula Botanical
Gardens
Kama'ole Beach Park
Keawakapu Beach Park
Polipoli Springs
State Recreation Area
Wailea Beach Park
WAILEA
Tedeschi
Winery
MAKENA
Makena-La Perouse Bay
State Park

LA PEROUSE BAY

KANAIO BEACH
KANALOA
POINT

ISLAND OF MAUI

· ·

- Known as the "Valley Isle."

- 727.3 square miles.

- Population: 127,000

- Average temperature: 71 degrees F in January-February, 78 degrees F in August-September.

- National parks: 2; State parks: 13; County parks: 107.

- Famed for whale-watching excursions, world-class windsurfing, marine-related and fine art productions.

- Warm, dry climate in beach areas, semitropical and wet on windward mountain slopes. Atop Haleakala (alt. 10,023 feet): occasionally below freezing in the winter months, with snow.

- Average annual rainfall: 15 inches in Lahaina, 69 inches in Hana.

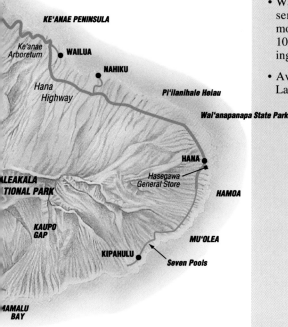

KE'ANAE PENINSULA

Ke'anae Arboretum

WAILUA

NAHIKU

Hana Highway

Pi'ilanihale Heiau

Wai'anapanapa State Park

HANA

Hasegawa General Store

HAMOA

HALEAKALA NATIONAL PARK

KAUPO GAP

MU'OLEA

KIPAHULU

Seven Pools

MAMALU BAY

Hana Coast

Second in size in the Hawaiian chain, Maui is one of Polynesia's principal "high islands," dominated by the massive shoulders of 10,023-foot Haleakala and mile-high Puu Kukui, "candlenut mountain," volcanoes. Named for the trickster demigod of Polynesian lore, Maui defers only to Oahu in visitor popularity and economic vigor.

The latter is a relatively new development. Although it was a powerful, resource-rich rival to the Big Island before Europeans came, Maui lost much of its influence when commerce flowed to deeper, safer Honolulu harbor in the nineteenth century. The transfer of the Hawaiian monarchy from Lahaina Town to Honolulu in 1843 symbolized this decline of power.

Important in mid-century as a center of missionary influence, and as a rowdy "rest and recreation" port for wintering whalers back from the North Pacific, Lahaina by 1900 had lapsed into gritty, red-soil sugar cultivation. The rest of the island followed as sugar, pineapple and even rubber plantations were established in Wailuku Hana, Puunene, Olowalu, Haiku, Nahiku

The lokelani—Maui's flower

and a dozen other towns. Chief among these were the holdings of Sam Alexander and Henry Perrine Baldwin, both Lahaina missionary sons, who hired Chinese to build an astonishing network of canals, tunnels and dams to bring water from East Maui streams to the island's barren, sandy "saddle." That former desert is now the heart of Alexander & Baldwin's 36,000-acre Hawaiian Commercial & Sugar Company plantation, Hawaii's largest and most profitable.

About the same time, descendants of missionary Edward P. Bailey used a similar catchment system to bring the waters of Puu Kukui's four chief rivers to the West Maui land that today is devoted to pineapple, macadamia nuts, housing developments, resort hotels and golf courses.

The recent economic diversification of Maui's family-held plantations and ranch lands has spun off several world-class beach resorts: Kaanapali out of Pioneer Mill property, Wailea on Alexander & Baldwin acreage once owned by Matson Navigation Col., Kapalua out of Maui Pineapple Company, and

Matson Navigation Co., Kapalua out of Maui Pineapple Company, and the new Makena Prince resort built by Japanese on Ulupalakua Ranch.

Similarly, land once part of Hana Ranch now cradles the Hotel Hana Maui, and the fast-growing Kihei residential community is sited on former Haleakala Ranch acreage.

"Fast-growing" applies to all of Maui as the twenty-first century nears. With cool upland vistas and miles of sunny leeward beachfront, Maui in the 1960s and 1970s catapulted out of dormancy to become one of the world's choicest resort investments. Property values started soaring 40 percent a year, and the island soon boasted of more millionaires per capita than the French Riviera.

While the boomtown mentality unleashed by this real estate frenzy has taken a toll of Maui's reputation as *no ka oi*, "the best," the island is still underpopulated in comparison with Oahu. It probably will continue, however, to absorb the lion's share of the State's new growth.

1. The winding curves to
   Haleakala
2. A scenic ride

Maui's geography is dominated by dormant Haleakala and its slopes, a broad central isthmus, and the compact West Maui mountains. Four sample tours give a good sense of Maui's diversity.

1. HALEAKALA AND UPCOUNTRY

The drive up 10,023-foot Haleakala and the view from the top are among the best reasons to visit Maui. Starting in Kahului, take Kula Road (Route 37) and Haleakala Highway, marveling as you climb past pineapple and sugar-cane fields, ranchlands, emerald-green truck farms, rain forests, mist-wrapped eucalyptus stands, high grasslands and, above the clouds, the alpine shrubs and barren deserts of the summit.

The Haleakala National Park visitor center perches above Haleakala Crater, a vast landscape of cinder slopes and multicolor volcanic cones floating on a sea of clouds. Off to the southeast are the volcanic peaks of the Big Island and, far below to the west, the lesser islands of Kahoolawe, Lanai, Molokai and, on clear days, Oahu.

Watching the sunrise (or sunset) from the summit is a Maui tradition. After the spectacle, go to the park visitor center to learn the lore of Haleakala and to look at Maui's unique silversword plant.

Head down Haleakala Highway (carefully!) to Kula and its Botanical Garden for the exotic protea plants. For a taste of Hawaiian wine, stop at Tedeschi Winery. This is "upcountry" Maui, perpetually green and glorious. Enjoy a leisurely lunch in Kula or in the ranching town of Makawao.

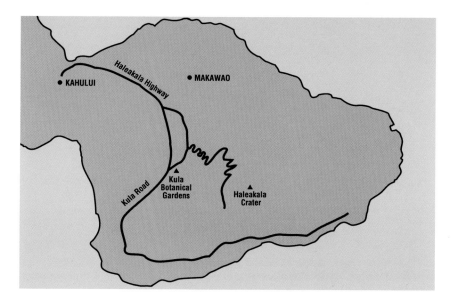

2. HANA AND THE NORTHEAST COAST

Set aside a day for this. Take a swimsuit, a towel, a supply of dramamine, and umbrella or rain coat —just in case. This is the wettest part of Maui.

Start at Paia, the wind-surfing headquarters just outside Kahului and a good place for breakfast. Paia is also your last chance to fill your gas tank. Nearby Hookipa Beach Park is where good wind-surfing enthusiasts go.

Then buckle up for a succession of twists, turns, and wondrous vistas along the narrow 52-mile Hana Highway. Untainted landscapes around every corner, waterfalls by the score, 56 bridges, and rich tropical vegeta-tion are the special pleasures of this trip. Keanae Arboretum, Waianapanapa State Park and Caves, and several private gardens are good stops along the way. Take your time. Stop frequently to enjoy the peaceful fertility of Hawaii's own Eden.

One of Hawaii's loveliest and most remote outposts, the village of Hana is a relaxing lunch stop after the dizzying drive. Check the friendly Hana Cultural Center (Hale Waiwai o Hana). (The legendary Hasegawa General Store burned in 1990.) Go to the Hana Bay shorefront for a look at offshore Alau Island. Then on to Hamoa Beach, Wailua Falls and finally the Seven Pools of Kipahulu for a refreshing fresh-water swim before starting the long drive back.

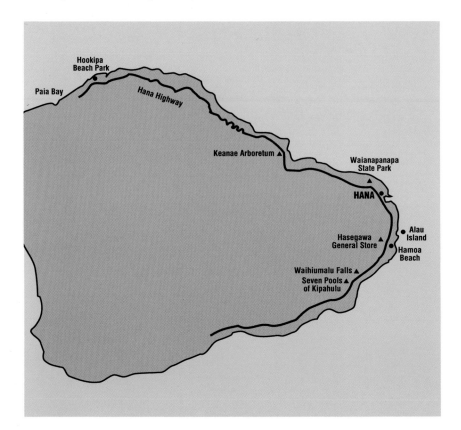

1. Enchanting Gardens
2. Alau Island
3. Keanae
4. Hookipa

3. CENTRAL AND SOUTH MAUI

Wailuku and Kahului are twin towns set in the center of the island, between the West Maui mountains and the north coast. Wailuku, the Maui county seat, is older; Kahului is a growing port town with three shopping malls. Important stops include Maui's oldest existing Christian place of worship, Kaahumanu Church on High Street in Wailuku; Maui Botanical Garden; Iao Valley State Park; Iao Needle; and the Alexander & Baldwin Sugar Museum in nearby Puunene.

The dry, sun-drenched south coast of Maui features Kihei's large condominium apartments and small hotels, and the manicured resorts and golf courses at Wailea and Makena.

The best-known beaches are Makena's Big Beach and Little Beach. Despite State laws, the latter is frequented by those who like to sunbathe all over, a habit persisting from the 1970s when tent cities were set up in the dry forest behind the Makena beaches. Offshore is barren Kahoolawe island, the subject of an on-going "discussion" between Hawaiian activists and the U.S. Navy over use of the now-uninhabited island for bombing practice. Makena is the end of the road for all but four-wheel-drive vehicles.

The south coast from Kihei to Makena is known for top-notch sailing, snorkeling and scuba diving. If you are a diver, join a tour to Molokini Islet, a little volcanic cone about three miles off this coast.

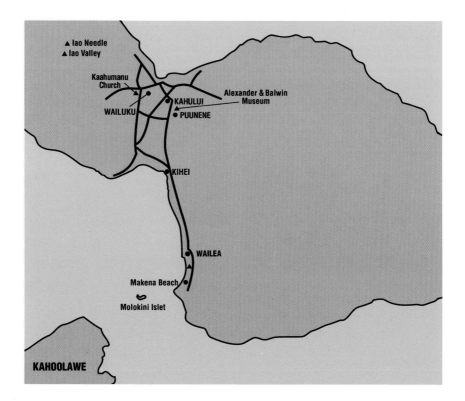

1. *Kihei*
2. *Maui Tropical Plantation*
3. *Grand Wailea Resort & Spa*
4. *Wailuku-Kahului*

105

4. WEST MAUI

Lahaina is an old whaling town transformed into a bustling center for tourists, shoppers and nighttime revelers. In fact, the rowdy action along Front Street today is no more than an update on Lahaina's notorious past, when New England whalers came ashore after months at sea.

On Front Street start at the venerable Pioneer Inn (it has one of the best bars in the Pacific). The brig *Carthaginian II*, a replica of a Yankee whaler, is moored in front. Right next door are Hawaii's largest banyan tree and two structures of note: Baldwin House, built in 1832 and Maui's oldest building, now a museum of missionary memorabilia; and the coral-stone Hale Paahao prison, built in 1851 to handle too-boisterous sailors. Front Street proper, which runs along the water, is chock-a-block with busy shops, bars, art galleries and restaurants.

You can either drive to the nearby Kaanapali resort or take the restored Lahaina-Kaanapali & Pacific Railroad to the center of Kaanapali for a walking tour of the deluxe hotels lining this stretch of perfect beach. Tour the Whaler's Village restaurants, shops and museum.

Beyond Kaanapali is the beautifully designed Kapalua resort complex, worth a visit for its crystal-clear beaches, striking golf courses, rows of tall Norfolk Island pines, dramatic views across Pailolo Channel to the steep slopes of Molokai, and gourmet food.

Kapalua is the end of the road for rental cars; only four-wheel-drive vehicles are equipped for the bumpy trip around the northwest corner of West Maui to Waiehu and Kahului.

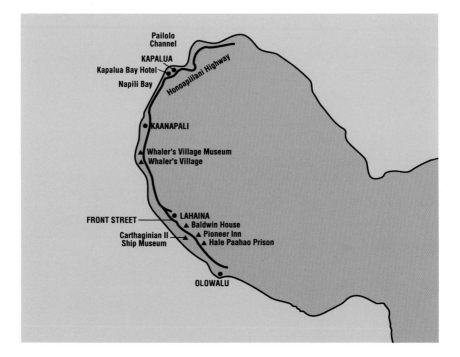

1. Kaanapali
2. Kapalua
3. Hawaii's largest banyan tree
4. Lahaina

West Maui Mountains

ALEXANDER & BALDWIN SUGAR MUSEUM

Puunene Sugar Mill

This cultural museum and gift shop housed near the historic Puunene sugar mill has artifacts, photos, and displays about sugar and plantation life. Open Monday through Saturday, 9:30 a.m. to 4 p.m. Adults, $2; children, $1. Located on Hansen Road, Puunene. Call 871-8058.

ALII GARDENS

Private, seven acres. Along Hana Highway near Hana Airport, this garden contains general lowland trees with extensive ginger and heliconia. Access is through the Hotel Hana Maui or with Temptation Tours. Call 248-7217 for information.

BAILEY HOUSE

This is a historic missionary home with Hawaiian artifacts, antique furniture, a gift shop and gallery. Open Monday through Saturday, 10 a.m. to 4:30 p.m. Closed holidays. Suggested donation for adults, $2; students, 50 cents. 2375-A Main Street, Wailuku. Call 244-3326 for information.

Gallery and gifts

DIVING

Like Honolulu's Hanauma Bay or the Big Island's Kealakekua Bay, Maui has its special diving site: Molokini Islet off Wailea. Parties are organized through dive shops or you can charter a boat at Maalaea.

Makena Beach (also on the south side), Black Rock at Kaanapali, Kapalua Bay, and the 14-mile marker on Honoapiilani Highway near Olowalu on the west side all are worth consideration, too.

FLEMING BEACH

A West Maui jewel

Excellent for picnicking, this beach was named for David Thomas Fleming, an early manager of Honolua Ranch and Baldwin Packers, who later developed Kapalua Beach as a public park. North of Kaanapali along Route 30.

HALEAKALA NATIONAL PARK

Last erupted circa 1797

Haleakala, "house of the sun," is 10,023 feet high. The national park of which this is the centerpiece in Upcountry Maui covers 27,350 acres. Seventeen-square-mile Haleakala Crater, greatly enlarged by erosion since its volcanic days, is 3,000 feet deep, 7.5 miles long, 2.5 miles wide, and 21 miles around the rim.

Haleakala is the home of the silversword plant and the nene goose, both endangered species endemic to Hawaii.

Watching the sunrise from the summit of Haleakala is a tradition on Maui. You'll have to sacrifice some sleep, however. Plan on hitting the road at 3:30 a.m. (4:30 a.m. is OK in mid-winter) for the two-hour drive to the summit in time for the pre-sunrise aurora. Dress warm: this means long pants, a sweater, and a jacket. Bring a blanket, just in case it's freezing up there.

Take Haleakala Highway (Route 37) out of Kahului, then Route 377 at Pukalani. Route 378 leads to the national park headquarters and the crater.

Haleakala National Park facilities usually are open 5:30 a.m. to 4:30 p.m. Entrance fee is $3 per car. Call the ranger station, 572-7749, for recorded park and weather information.

Tips:

•*Check the Maui papers for sunrise or sunset time on the day you plan to be there.*

•*Call the National Weather Service, 871-5054, to double check the weather.*

•*Take warm clothing for a sunrise visit; pre-dawn temperatures usually range from 42.6°F to 50°F, but they have gone to 14°F!*

•*Be careful of over-exertion at higher altitudes if you have a medical problem.*

•*Gas up the car and eat before departing.*

•*Tour companies will pick you up, transport you to the summit for sunrise, then provide bikes for you to coast the 10,000 feet down to Paia at the bottom.*

HAMOA BEACH

Hana surf spot

Although this 1,000-foot-long beach, a favorite surfing spot since the days of ancient Hawaiian chiefs, is open to the public, to gain access you must pass through Hana Ranch Company property. Ask at the Hotel Hana Maui. Hamoa Beach is off Hana Highway (Route 31) past Hana.

HANA

A Maui must

The long and winding road

You will need at least half a day each way to drive the approximately 52 miles over the famous Hana Highway, but what an experience!

This highway of twists and turns is lined with waterfalls, ferns, guava, breadfruit, and much scenery. Stop to sniff the fragrant flowers, admire the lush countryside, and marvel at the more than 600 turns, fifty-some bridges, and many one-lane stretches.

After a break at Hana to restore your composure, continue to the Seven Pools of Kipahulu (tour bro-chures call it "Seven Sacred Pools") and don't forget to use your camera.

To reach Hana, pick up Route 36 right outside Kahului Airport and stay on it. The same highway will take you to Wailua Falls and Kipahulu, beyond Hana.

Tips:
•*Tap your horn when approaching the highway's blind curves.*
•*Take along a copy of* Maui's Hana Highway *by noted biologist and Hawaiiana expert, Angela Kay Kepler.*
•*Start back early in the afternoon. You want to be on straight, paved highway before dark.*

HANA CULTURAL CENTER (HALE WAIWAI O HANA)

These historic buildings house Hana artifacts, photos, and documents. Open 10 a.m. to 4 p.m. Suggested donation is $2. Uakea Road in Hana. Call 248-8622.

HELANI GARDENS

Private, 70 acres. This one has extensive tropical foliage, ginger, and heliconia. You can tour the gardens on foot or by car. Open daily. Admission is $2 per person. One mile north of Hana, on the Hana Highway. Call 248-8274.

HOOKIPA BEACH PARK

The ultimate wind-surfing spot, Hookipa ("hospitality") Beach Park is the site of international competitions. The small sand strip with a rocky shelf is all that the 1946 tsunami left of a wide beach. Be careful of the ocean currents; check with the lifeguard before entering the water. On Hana Highway (Route 33) a few miles out of Kahului, just past Paia (the last chance to gas up before Hana).

Hookipa—board sailing mecca

IAO NEEDLE AND VALLEY

Prime photo candidate

Just outside Wailuku, about seven miles from Kahului Airport, is Iao Valley, the scene of a ferocious battle between the forces of Kamehameha the Great and the chiefs of Maui. At the end, so many were dead that the waters of Iao Stream ran red with blood. Nearby Wailuku, "water of destruction," got its name from the battle. Iao Needle, at 2,250 feet, (686 meters), is the fourth highest peak on Maui and a prime candidate for your photo album. Take Kaahumanu Avenue (Route 32) through Wailuku (it becomes Iao Valley Road) to Iao Park. Stop at Kepaniwai Gardens and the John Kennedy Profile along the way.

KAAHUMANU CHURCH

Maui's oldest

Built in 1837 of plastered stone, Kaahumanu Church is the oldest existing Christian church on Maui. It was named for the Maui-born favorite wife of Kamehameha the Great, Queen Kaahumanu. On High Street (Route 30), at the southwest edge of Wailuku, six miles from Kahului Airport.

KAANAPALI COAST

Maui's Riviera

One of the major resort areas in Hawaii, Kaanapali on the west coast of Maui has six luxury hotels; two par 72 golf courses, including the championship Royal Kaanapali; numerous condominium developments; tennis courts galore, and three miles of the whitest beaches you will ever see. Until the early 1960s, this area was mostly cane field and *kiawe* (mesquite). Ride the Lahaina-Kaanapali & Pacific Railroad while you're there. Kaanapali is on the Honoapiilani Highway (Route 30) about an hour from Kahului Airport.

KAHULUI

Port of call

Kahului is the main point of entry for visitors to Maui. It has the principal airport and the only deep-water port on the island, through which Maui's sugar and pineapples are shipped. Check out Kanaha Pond Wildlife Sanctuary. Try the *guri-guri* sherbet at Tasaka's Guri-Guri Shop in the Maui Mall.

KAPALUA

Embracing the sea

North of Kaanapali on the west coast of Maui, just past Napili Bay, is Kapalua ("arms embracing the sea" is one translation), another major resort destination. It has the Kapalua Bay Hotel and Villas, two championship golf courses, tennis and water sport facilities, restaurants, and shops. On the Honoapiilani Highway (Route 30), approximately an hour from Kahului Airport.

KEANAE ARBORETUM

Public, free, five acres. Tropical trees, *taro* collection, fruit trees, palms, bamboo, etc. Thirty-two miles east of Kahului on Hana Highway, near the Keanae YMCA. Call 248-8592.

KEPANIWAI PARK

Public, free, eight acres. This convenient park is especially good for picnics, and emphasizes the major ethnic groups in Hawaii with matching architecture and plants. En route to Iao Valley State Monument.

KIHEI

Best bet for sun

A sun-drenched ten-mile stretch of Maui's south coast, Kihei, "cloak," in the past decade has acquired numerous hotels and rental condos. Snorkeling, scuba diving, swimming and sailing are popular here. Come prepared for sun; Kihei is in the sunniest part of Maui with annual rainfall of only 13 inches. It's all on Mokulele Highway (Route 350) and Kihei Road, about nine miles south of Kahului Airport.

KULA

Cool Kula

The most diversified harvests in Hawaii probably come from Kula. Sweet Maui onions, cabbages, potatoes, tomatoes, fruit, wine grapes, flowers, cattle and more grow well in this cool climate. Along the Haleakala Highway (Route 37), about 20 miles from Kahului Airport.

Tip: Check out the Kula Botanical Garden and Sunrise Protea Farm. The protea is a fascinating flower, fresh or dried.

KULA BOTANICAL GARDEN

A verdant visit

Private, five acres. Trees, shrubs, and proteas grow here. Open 9 a.m. to 4 p.m. Teens and adults, $4; children 6 through 12, $1. On Highway 377 in Kula. Call 878-1715.

LAHAINA

Former whaling capital

Lahaina, "merciless sun," is well named. A one-time whaling town on the west end of Maui, today it is a favorite visitor destination. King Kamehameha I made Lahaina his capital after he consolidated the Islands into one kingdom in 1790. The seat of power remained here until Kamehameha III moved it to Honolulu in 1845.

This is a good place for walking, so wear comfortable shoes! Front Street, Pioneer Mill, Lahaina Harbor and *Carthaginian II*, Hale Paahao ("whaler's brig"), and the Baldwin House all are within a block or two of the Pioneer Inn and its banyan tree.

Take Route 380 out of Kahului to Honoapiilani Highway (Route 30), which will take you directly to Lahaina, Kaanapali, and Kapalua, a distance of about 25 miles.

Lahaina Restoration Foundation on Dickenson and Front Streets is involved in historic buildings, including the Baldwin House, the Wo Hing Chinese Temple, and Hale Paahao Prison. Furnishings, artifacts, and photos are on display. Library, gift shop, reading room attached, and tours are available. Call 661-3262.

LA PEROUSE BAY

A wind swept, rocky shore

The first westerner known to have set foot on Maui, the French explorer Jean Francois de Galaup, Count de la Perouse, came ashore here on May 30, 1786. The fishing is good on this rocky beach, but heavy trade-wind surf makes swimming dangerous. The bay is at the end of the road, close to the southernmost tip of Maui, past Kihei and Wailea.

MAKAWAO

Cowboy traditions

Upcountry Makawao, "eye of dawn," has a proud cowboy heritage. Originally a community of plantation and cattle-ranch workers, it is now a thriving little retail center. The Fourth of July rodeo at Oskie Rice Arena is one of Maui's most popular events. Take Route 380 out of Kahului to Haleakala Highway (Route 37), then follow Makawao Avenue (Route 400).

MAUI THE DEMIGOD

An impish foster child   Ralph Kagehiro

The island seems to have taken its name from an adventuresome Polynesian spirit who frolicks his way through many Hawaiian folk tales. Maui "the trickster," a foster son of the gods, learned their magic and then taunted them with it. A rascal who defied mighty chiefs, he played pranks and outwitted gods, goddesses and all in lesser authority.

Hawaiian legend says that among Maui's great feats was the creation of the island of Maui by pulling it up from the sea floor. He also lassoed the sun that once upon a time raced across the sky so fast that the *kapa* (bark cloth) Maui's mother was making would not dry. Catching the sun, Maui convinced it to move more slowly. His mother's *kapa* then dried properly, thanks to the longer day.

MAUI BOTANICAL GARDEN

Public, free, three acres. Native Hawaiian plants, especially hibiscus and Polynesian introductions, are here for viewing. In Kahului, at Wailuku Zoo near Kaahumanu Shopping Center.

MAUI TROPICAL PLANTATION

This popular stop, a 120-acre working plantation, grows island plants such as sugar cane, bananas, pineapple, star fruit, anthuriums, orchids, and guava. The Plantation's restaurant is as pleasant as its gardens. Open 9 a.m. to 5 p.m.. Free. In Waikapu, just south of Kahului. Call 244-7643 for information; 242-8605 for reservations.

MOLOKINI ISLET

A diver's delight

A small cinder cone lifting its head 160 feet from the sea south of Maui, Molokini Islet has only 18.6 acres. Half of the crater rim has been eroded away. Because its underwater slope is steep, several marine ecosystems exist within a very compact space, making it a unique diving experience.

Molokini is a protected marine life conservation district.

PIONEER INN

Lahaina landmark

Built in 1901, the "must-see" Pioneer Inn fronts Wharf Street in Lahaina. Stroll around the courtyard and read the original house rules on the wall. The banyan tree across the street, the largest in the islands, covers two-thirds of an acre. It was planted in 1873 to commemorate the fiftieth anniversary of the first Protestant mission at Lahaina.

PROTEA

Versatile flower

Originally from Australia and South Africa, but finding ideal growing conditions on the slopes of Haleakala, the protea flower comes in many shapes, sizes, and colors. Whether fresh or dried, it makes an excellent gift.

SEVEN POOLS OF KIPAHULU

An island idyll

At journey's end on Hana Highway (Route 36) about 60 miles out of Kahului, Seven Pools (often called "the seven sacred pools" with more hyperbole than basis in tradition) is a place for quiet reflection amid waterfalls, great swimming in crystal clear waters, and perfect pictures.

SILVERSWORD

The desert's gray daisy

A member of the daisy family, *Argyroxiphium sandwicense* ("silversword of the Sandwich Islands") is unique to Haleakala. (A closely related and equally scarce species survives precariously atop the West Maui mountains.) Its silver comes from thick fine white hairs, which protect the plant from the sun and wind. Ancient Hawaiians called it *ahinahina*, gray hair. Surviving in desert environments, it can take 20 years to send up its only flower stalk. Silverswords are endangered, so do not touch the plants. And please stay on the trails while visiting Haleakala; inadvertent trampling can kill tiny silversword seedlings.

ULUPALAKUA RANCH

Fine wine

In addition to raising cattle and sheep on more than 20,000 acres on the slopes of Haleakala, this ranch is becoming known as wine country, thanks to recent experiments with Carnelian grapes. A partnership between Ulupalakua Ranch owner C. Pardee Erdman and Napa Valley-born Emil Tedeschi led to establishment of Tedeschi Winery, which now markets Maui Nouveau, pineapple wine, and *blanc de noir* champagne.

UPCOUNTRY

On Maui, "Upcountry" means Pukalani, Makawao and Kula towns, and the lower slopes of Haleakala. The cooler temperatures at these altitudes are excellent for growing protea flowers and vegetables.

Flower farming

WAIANAPANAPA STATE PARK AND CAVES

Crystal water tubes

Three miles from Hana, this state park is best known for the Waianapanapa, "glistening water," Caves. Like the Thurston Lava Tube on the Big Island, these caves were formed when a stream of lava cooled on the surface while the still molten interior flowed out, leaving a tube. The caves hold crystal clear water, which at certain times of the year turns red with millions of tiny shrimp. The color is said to be a reminder of a princess, slain by her cruel husband after fleeing and taking refuge in the caves.

The park also has a black-sand beach and camping facilities, with cabins. It's all on the Hana Highway (Route 36) about 49 miles out of Kahului.

WAILEA

Desert turned deluxe

This deluxe resort area 17 miles from Kahului on the southeast coast, just south of Kihei, was a brush and cactus desert until the 1970s. With water Wailea has been transformed into an exclusive, tasteful, and much-sought-after resort complete with world-class hotels and acres of golf courses. As in Kihei, expect a lot of sun. The area gets only ten inches of rain a year. Take Mokulele Highway (Route 350) out of Kahului, then the Piilani Highway (Route 31) through Kihei.

WAILUA FALLS

Hana meets Hollywood

Wailua Falls was filmed extensively in MGM's version of the classic, *Mutiny on the Bounty*. On the Hana Highway, you'll find it just before the Seven Pools of Kipahulu, about 57 miles out of Kahului.

WAILUKU

Hawaiian battleground

Wailuku ("waters [of] destruction"), Maui's county seat, earned its name in 1790, when Kamehameha the Great waged a ferocious battle against rival Maui chiefs in neighboring Iao Valley. So many died that the stream ran red with blood. Visit Kaahumanu Church, Bailey House, and Iao Park while you are in Wailuku.

WEST MAUI MOUNTAINS

Craggy peaks and valleys

Puu Kukui, the older of Maui's two volcanoes, formed the west massif of the island eons ago. Stream erosion has carved this craggy landscape into sharp peaks and deep valleys. Lava from Haleakala, the newer and larger volcano, merged with flows from the West Maui mountains to create the large, central isthmus from which Maui derived its familiar name, "the Valley Isle."

WHALER'S VILLAGE MUSEUM

A look back into the past

An enjoyable display in Kaanapali's Whalers Village shopping complex, with artifacts, photos, and gift shop. Open 9:30 a.m. to 10 p.m. Free. Call 661-5992.

ISLAND OF MOLOKAI

- Known as the "Friendly Isle."
- 260.0 square miles which include 13.2 square miles of Kalawao County (a State-administered hospital settlement).
- Major industries: diversified agriculture, tourism, cattle ranching.
- Kalawao County (a State-administered hospital settlement): 13.3 square miles.
- Population: 6,800.

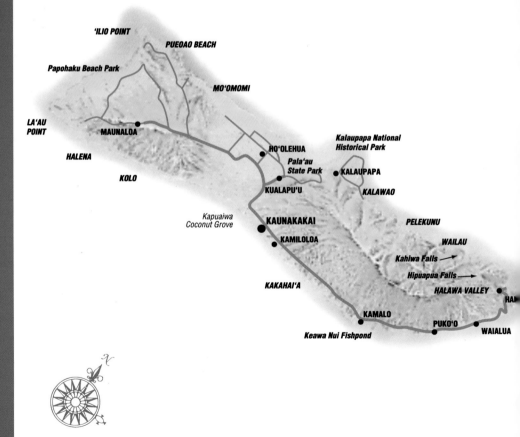

'ILIO POINT

PUEOAO BEACH

Papohaku Beach Park

MO'OMOMI

LA'AU POINT

MAUNALOA

Kalaupapa National Historical Park

HALENA

HO'OLEHUA

Pala'au State Park

KALAUPAPA

KOLO

KUALAPU'U

KALAWAO

Kapuaiwa Coconut Grove

KAUNAKAKAI

PELEKUNU

KAMILOLOA

WAILAU

Kahiwa Falls

Hipuapua Falls

KAKAHAI'A

HALAWA VALLEY

HA

KAMALO

PUKO'O

WAIALUA

Keawa Nui Fishpond

The correct positioning of Molokai has been adjusted for viewing purposes.

acred to the goddess Hina, and the legendary home of Hawaii's greatest healers and sorcerers, Molokai remains a tranquil, rural buffer between powerful Oahu (Honolulu) and booming Maui. Casting uneasy glances at its hyperactive neighbors, the sparsely populated "Friendly Isle" thus far has resisted tourist development, preferring the low-profile role of country cousin. There are no discos on Molokai.

Although its size and mountainous terrain would seemingly lump Molokai with the big islands of Hawaii, Maui, Oahu and Kauai, the island's rural values and the survival skills of its residents bespeak a closer kinship with Lanai and Niihau. With an economy that has been moribund for decades, Molokai produces more than its share of hunters, fishermen and farmers.

It also has the State's most prominent ethnic Hawaiian community, due in part to the substantial Hawaiian Homestead acreage at Hoolehua. Of Molokai's seven thousand residents, about five thousand classify themselves as Hawaiian or part-Hawaiian, a ratio exceeded only on tiny Niihau. Farming, fishing and tourism are the principal dollar earners.

The island is dominated by two great ranches—arid Molokai Ranch on the western half, and rainy Puu o Hoku ("hill of stars") Ranch in the east. In between are mile-high mountains, vast inaccessible valleys, and some of Hawaii's broadest reefs. Locked up for years by Molokai Ranch, the splendid coves and beaches of Molokai's West End were finally opened to the public late in the 1970s with the development of the Kaluakoi Resort near three-mile-long Papohaku Beach.

The wide main street, low-rise frontier architecture and tranquil harbor of Kaunakakai, the only town, recall the leisurely Polynesia of Nordhoff and Hall rather than the go-go Hawaii of Tom Selleck. A royal coconut grove and crowded "church row" fortify the bucolic impression.

On the island's wild and spectacular north shore opposite Kaunakakai is the famous Kalaupapa settlement where Father Damien de Veuster spent his last years aiding Hawaii's abandoned nineteenth century leprosy patients. Situated on a low peninsula guarded by some of the world's loftiest sea cliffs, Kalaupapa is a unique and soul-stirring community.

Kukui flower representing Molokai

MOLOKAI FACTS

BEACHES

Nearly empty strands

Papohaku Beach, ten miles from the airport on the west end of the island, is the quintessential Hawaiian beach. Although massive 6,700-acre Kaluakoi Resort is nearby, Papohaku is often empty. Also on the west end is idyllic Kawakiu Beach, the place for snorkeling and swimming.

DINING

Kaluakoi resort has restaurants, but also try the Kanemitsu Bakery (famous for its "Molokai Bread"), the Pau Haua Inn and the Mid Nite Inn. All are in Kaunakakai. Where else?

GOLF

In addition to a rustic nine-hole course at Kalae there is an 18-hole, 6,618-yard links at Kaluakoi Resort at the west end of the island. Open weekdays, 7:30 a.m. to 6 p.m.; weekends, 7 a.m. to 6 p.m. Green fee is $40 if you stay at the resort, $55 if you do not. Call 552-2739 for reservations and information.

Kaluakoi golfing

HALAWA VALLEY

Ancient habitation

Four miles long and half a mile wide, Halawa Valley has the oldest recorded habitation site (circa A.D. 650) on Molokai. Once a large fishing and farming community, Halawa never recovered from the devastating 1946 tidal wave which wreaked havoc throughout the Hawaiian Islands.

KALAUPAPA NATIONAL HISTORICAL PARK

Jointly managed by the Hawaii State Department of Health and the National Park Service, this isolated settlement for Hansen's Disease patients can be viewed from the Palaau State Park Lookout. You can, of course, hike the three-mile trail that drops about 2,000 feet to the Kalaupapa peninsula, but plan on three hours to come back up.

Taking the Molokai Mule Ride is a bit easier and more popular. It traverses the 26 switchbacks every day but Sunday. The mules are sure-footed, and the view is terrific. Allow a full day for this trip and dress comfortably, preferably in long pants.

The required permission from the Hawaii Department of Health to visit the settlement can be obtained through the local tour companies. Write Kalaupapa National Historical Park, Kalaupapa, Hawaii 96742.

Hansen's is a chronic, infectious disease that affects the skin, eyes, and nerves. Caused by the bacterium *Mycobacterium leprae*, it was described as early as 1500 B.C. It is transmitted through direct, usually prolonged re-petitive contact. Actually, it is one of the least contagious of communicable diseases, with only 4 to 5 percent of the world's population even susceptible to it.

Until sulfone drugs brought leprosy under control in the late 1940s, patients in Hawaii were banished to Kalaupapa settlement. Although leprosy is now recognized as completely controllable and isolation is a thing of the past, a few dozen patients remain there voluntarily. Visitors frequently comment on the community's complete absence of youngsters and on the numerous pets.

a thing of the past, a few dozen patients remain there voluntarily. Visitors frequently comment on the community's complete absence of youngsters and on the numerous pets.

1

2

1. Kalaupapa village
2. Kalaupapa National Historical Park today

KAWAKIU BEACH

Quiet aquatics

This idyllic place for snorkeling and swimming is on the west end of the island, close to Kaluakoi Resort.

KAUNAKAKAI

Rustic reminder

Molokai's population center, Kaunakakai is a colorful reminder of the 1930s, complete with horses tethered under the trees, a long wharf for agricultural exports, and a harbor where boats can be rented for fishing, sailing, snorkeling, diving, or whale-watching.

MOLOKAI RANCH

Creatures featured

The second largest cattle operation in the Hawaiian islands, controlling more than 56,000 acres, this ranch also runs the Molokai Ranch Wildlife Park. A 2,000-acre park with nearly five hundred animals from Asia and Africa, the park offers a pretty good Serengeti right here in Paradise.

NORTH SHORE

Cliffs of Molokai's north shore

Spectacular valleys, dense vegetation, cloud-scraping cliffs, silvery waterfalls plunging into the sea characterize the windward side of Molokai, but only Kalaupapa Peninsula and Halawa Valley are readily accessible. No roads approach the North Shore, only very rugged trails; the rest of the coast can be seen only from the air, from a kayak, or from a yacht.

SAINT PHILOMENA CHURCH

Circa 1890

This simple church stands where Father Joseph Damien de Veuster landed in 1873 to begin his humanitarian work with the leprosy victims of Kalaupapa. Father Damien's only shelter for weeks after his arrival was the pandanus tree next to the present church. Buried next to the tree 16 years later, his remains were subsequently returned to his native Belgium in 1936.

Former burial site

Father Damien's Church

TOURS

Damien Molokai Tours or Ike's Tours can arrange hiking or flying into Kalaupapa Settlement. Gray Line Molokai or Roberts Hawaii can help with general tours of the island.

ISLAND OF NIIHAU

- Nicknamed the "Forbidden Island."
- 69.9 square miles, privately owned.
- Native Hawaiians living a rural life.
- Only limited access by general public through helicopter landings, operated by the owners of the island, at uninhabited sites.
- Population: 230.

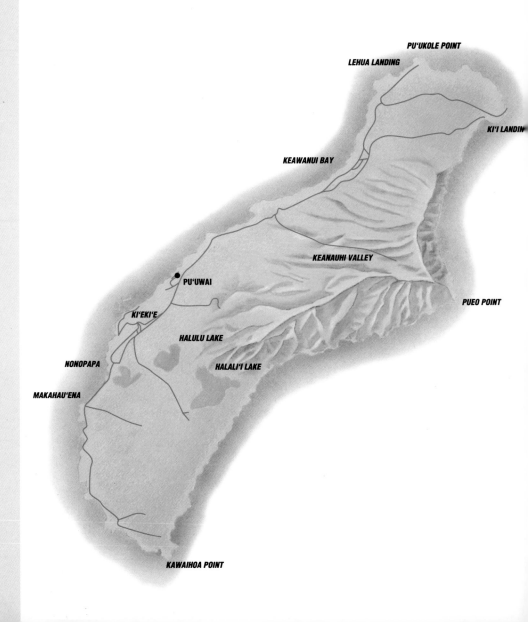

PU'UKOLE POINT

LEHUA LANDING

KI'I LANDIN

KEAWANUI BAY

KEANAUHI VALLEY

PU'UWAI

PUEO POINT

KI'EKI'E

HALULU LAKE

NONOPAPA

HALALI'I LAKE

MAKAHAU'ENA

KAWAIHOA POINT

Arid, low-lying Niihau is one of two privately owned islands in the Hawaiian chain. (Lanai, 99 percent owned by Castle & Cooke, is the other.) The Robinson family of Kauai, descendants of Mrs. Elizabeth Sinclair, who bought the island from King Kamehameha IV in the 1860s, are its guardians.

Today a preserve for Hawaiians who live by traditional values, Niihau has largely resisted the blandishments of tourism and materialism. The island has no hotels or shopping centers. Visitors come only by invitation of the Robinson family or a Niihau resident. The subsistence economy centers on fishing, small ranches, family farming, and stringing rare and costly necklaces of tiny colorful shells found on one Niihau beach. Although many of the island's 200 residents are at home with English, Hawaiian is their first language.

Past visitors to Niihau include Captain James Cook, who made a strenuous landing in 1778 in a quest for provisions for his ships, and a Japanese fighter pilot who crash-landed there following the 1941 Pearl Harbor attack.

Historically, Niihau has been dominated by nearby Kauai, since the two have been isolated from the islands to the east by the archipelago's widest and one of its most dangerous channels. Situated at the exposed northwestern end of the main Hawaiian group, Niihau receives thunderous storm surf and high winds during winter. Westward-sweeping ocean currents are a year-around threat.

In ancient times, Niihau people were known as mat weavers, yam farmers and independent thinkers.

Famous Niihau shell

1

2

3

4

5

1. *Treacherous coastline.*
2. *Rural community living.*
3. *Isolated beauty.*
4. *"Forbidden Island" sunset
   viewed from Kauai.*
5. *Shoreline cliff of Niihau.*

129

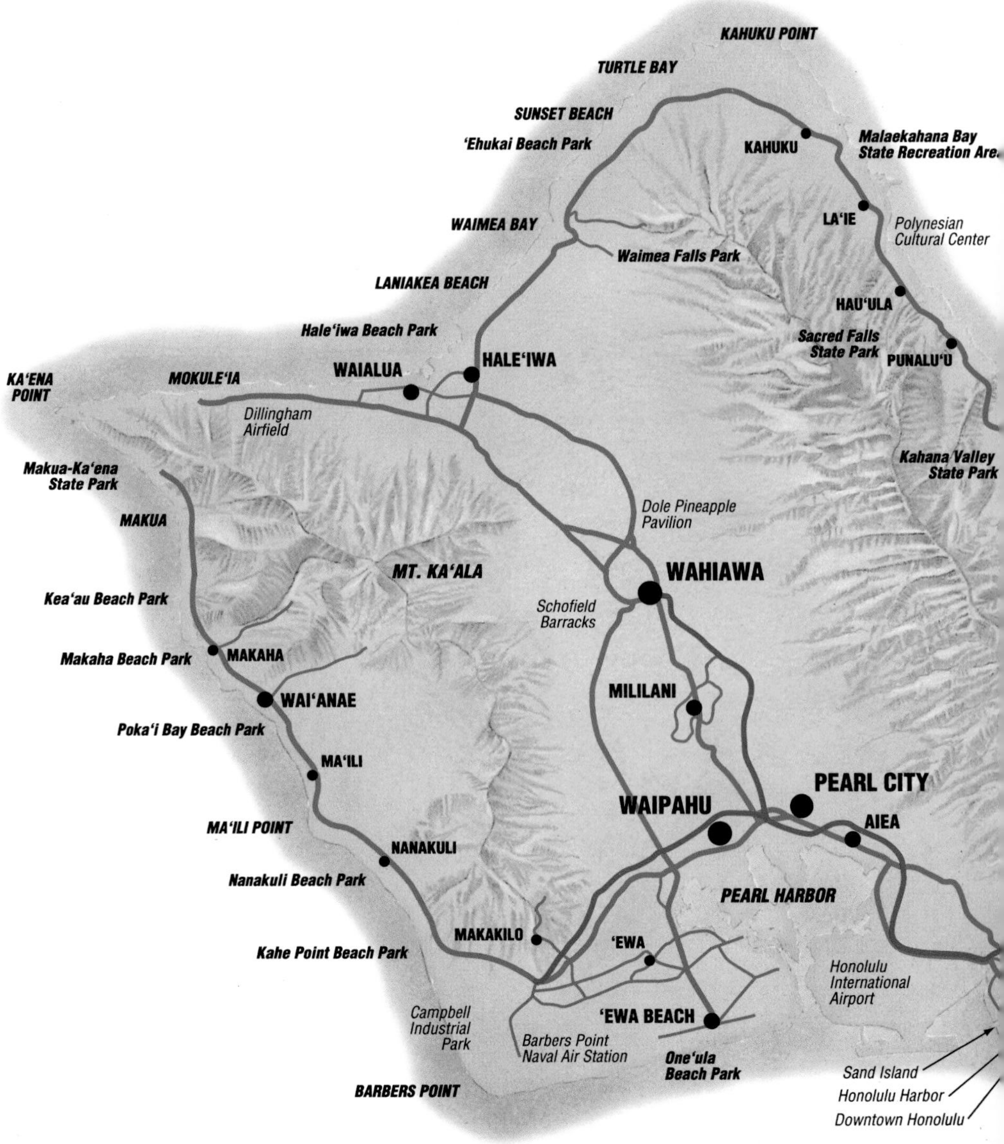

KAHUKU POINT

TURTLE BAY

SUNSET BEACH

'Ehukai Beach Park

KAHUKU

Malaekahana Bay
State Recreation Are.

LA'IE

Polynesian
Cultural Center

WAIMEA BAY

Waimea Falls Park

LANIAKEA BEACH

HAU'ULA

Hale'iwa Beach Park

Sacred Falls
State Park

PUNALU'U

MOKULE'IA

WAIALUA

HALE'IWA

KA'ENA
POINT

Dillingham
Airfield

Kahana Valley
State Park

Makua-Ka'ena
State Park

Dole Pineapple
Pavilion

MAKUA

MT. KA'ALA

WAHIAWA

Kea'au Beach Park

Schofield
Barracks

Makaha Beach Park

MAKAHA

WAI'ANAE

MILILANI

Poka'i Bay Beach Park

MA'ILI

PEARL CITY

WAIPAHU

MA'ILI POINT

AIEA

NANAKULI

Nanakuli Beach Park

PEARL HARBOR

MAKAKILO

'EWA

Kahe Point Beach Park

Honolulu
International
Airport

Campbell
Industrial
Park

'EWA BEACH

Barbers Point
Naval Air Station

One'ula
Beach Park

BARBERS POINT

Sand Island
Honolulu Harbor
Downtown Honolulu

ISLAND OF OAHU

• •

- The center of business and government for Hawaii.

- Second smallest of the four major islands in geographical size: 591 sq. land miles.

- Three-fourths of the State's population.

- Downtown Honolulu is Hawaii's financial center. Waikiki, the world-famous tourist destination, is only a few miles away.

- Resident population 865,000 including military personnel stationed or homeported on Oahu.

- Military personnel and dependents: Statewide, 117,141; Honolulu, 116,603. Military percentage of Oahu population: almost 14%.

- Major military installations: Pearl Harbor Naval Shipyard, Barbers Point Naval Air Station, Kaneohe Bay Marine Corps Air Station, Hickam Air Force Base, Tripler Army Medical Center, Fort Shafter (Army), Schofield Barracks (Army).

- Waikiki average temperature: 71.9 degrees F. in January-February, 80.6 degrees F. in August-September.

- Average annual rainfall: 20 inches in Waianae area, 158 inches in upper Manoa Valley.

- Attractions: sunny beaches, international shops and restaurants.

- Honolulu visitor arrivals: 5,049,000

- Hotel and apartment-hotel units: 38,022.

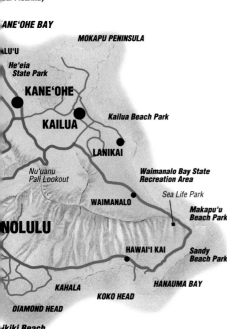

MAN'S HAT
OLI'I ISLAND)

ANE'OHE BAY

MOKAPU PENINSULA

LU'U

He'eia
State Park

KANE'OHE

KAILUA

Kailua Beach Park

LANIKAI

Nu'uanu
Pali Lookout

Waimanalo Bay State
Recreation Area

Sea Life Park

WAIMANALO

Makapu'u
Beach Park

NOLULU

HAWAI'I KAI

Sandy
Beach Park

KAHALA

HANAUMA BAY

KOKO HEAD

DIAMOND HEAD

ikiki Beach

Waikiki–gateway to Hawaii

While only third in size among the Hawaiian Islands, Oahu (synonymous these days with metropolitan Honolulu) was destined for paramountcy. The trading and whaling skippers that followed Captain James Cook in the late 1700s found on Oahu good natural harbors, bountiful fresh water, and a long, gentle lee anchorage for their sailing ships. Soon Oahu's relatively broad, arable coastal plains caught the eye of planters and ranchers.

Home today to 76 percent of the State's million-plus residents, Honolulu has been Hawaii's "gathering place" and its capital since Kamehameha III moved the monarchy here from Lahaina, Maui, in the 1840s. Favored by monarchs and travelers alike for a century and a half, Oahu is justly famous for its beaches, surf, wide bays, deep valleys, imposing cliffs, and the many islets and promontories that make it Hawaii's most picturesque island.

It is also the State's most economically and culturally diverse island. The huge visitor plant is supplemented by shipping, manufacturing, fi-nance, sugar and pineapple cultivation, oil refining, and the largest U.S. military bases in the Pacific. In addition, a heavy concentration of government, education and retail jobs has made Honolulu a magnet for job seekers.

Oahu is an island of remarkable contrasts: traffic jams and high rises on the Leeward side; banana groves and sugar cane fields on the Windward, and the jungly rain forest of Nuuanu is not far from the cactus-studded bluffs of Makaha.

The City and County of Honolulu (a single entity) covers the entire island.

Honolulu, with a large, diverse population and complex social structure, is a quilt of neighborhoods, some defined by valleys and ridges, others by economic or ethnic distinctions. Low-rise Kaimuki and adjacent high-rise Moiliili, both close to Waikiki, have been middle-class oriental neighborhoods since they were laid out in the 1920s. Kaimuki—particularly Waialae Avenue, its main thoroughfare, with small shops, hardware stores, "crack-seed" sellers and service

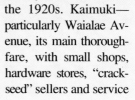

Oahu's flower—ilima

establishments—has the feel of pre-World War II Honolulu. The residential side streets feature simple homes on neat well-tended plots, showing enviable domestic pride.

The next-door Moiliili business district along King Street serves local residents and the nearby University of Hawaii community. Flower stalls, small medical offices, and health-food stores share the sidewalk frontage with copy services, banks, book nooks, a theater and ethnic restaurants.

As the State capital, Honolulu is certainly the most strikingly interesting city in the Pacific, as well as one of the most congested. Stretching for twenty-five miles along Oahu's leeward coast and into the misty Koolau foothills, Honolulu has dozens of diverse neighborhoods, hundreds of ethnic restaurants, and tens of thousands of hotel, condominium and high-rise apartment rooms.

Manoa, the large, deep valley behind the University of Hawaii, is interesting for its fine old homes, built early in the century by largely professional residents. Manoa's misty rains are responsible for frequent afternoon rainbows; the University of Hawaii athletic teams are the "Rainbows" or simply the "Bows."

Kahala and Waialae Iki, east of Diamond Head, get relatively little rain. They were once predominantly white suburbs, but local prosperity and investors from Japan have brought a new mix. Kalihi, on the opposite side of Downtown, is full of Hawaii's most recent immigrants and some of its older residents. Filipinos, Vietnamese, Cambodians, Koreans, and Samoans, as well as third-generation Japanese and native Hawaiians, share the turf in Kalihi, providing the best and cheapest ethnic food in Honolulu.

Chinatown, on the edge of the Downtown financial district, has been in transition since developers discovered the potential in restoring picturesque old neighborhoods.

The main campus of the University is here, as are the Honolulu Zoo, the Waikiki Aquarium, churches, hospitals, libraries, Federal and State buildings, sports facilities, theaters, and a dozen or more museums. Honolulu also has the only royal palace in the United States, and several prestigious private schools. All the State's major media outlets have their headquarters here, as do banks, airlines, and leading corporations.

Given Honolulu's dominant role in State affairs, it is little wonder that visitors sometimes mistakenly identify Oahu as the "big island"—a title that actually belongs to the more easterly island of Hawaii. But there is no question that Oahu is the pivot of the Hawaiian chain and will remain so despite official efforts to shift growth to the other islands. Oahu is where it all happens.

Two mountain ridges, the Koolaus to the east and the Waianae Range to the west, run roughly north to south the length of Oahu, with a broad central plain between them. Both are remnants of ancient volcanoes. Four comfortable day tours are sufficient to cover the island.

1. WINDWARD OAHU AND THE NORTH SHORE

A single day of driving with occasional stops will show Oahu's most notable scenery; you can revisit points of particular interest later if you wish.

From your Waikiki hotel, drive eastward on Kalakaua Avenue around Diamond Head and through the east Honolulu suburbs to Hanauma Bay, a famed (and crowded) beach formed long ago when one side of a volcanic crater collapsed into the sea. Although parking may be difficult, except early in the morning, be sure to stop at this picture-perfect bit of Polynesian scenery.

Beyond the bay is the dramatic southeast Oahu coastline with its dangerous Sandy Beach and Makapuu body-surfing areas. Makapuu Lookout surveys almost the entire Windward coast.

Follow the main highway past Waimanalo Beach State Park (it has one of the island's best beaches) and Mount Olomana to the bedroom communities of Kailua and Kaneohe. Northward, Oahu is at its tropical,

rural best. Scenic stops along the Kahekili and Kamehameha highways should include Haiku Garden, Valley of the Temples, Chinaman's Hat at Kualoa Park (for a marvelous view of Kaneohe Bay and the incredible Koolau escarpment), and lovely Kahana Bay. Just beyond little Punaluu community, a two-hour hike will get you in and out of Sacred Falls Valley. Take a swimsuit and towel for the pool beneath the falls, but first read the signs in the parking lot at the foot of the trail: Rain can cause extremely dangerous flash floods in the narrow valley.

At Laie see the Mormon Temple and the highly recommended Polynesian Cultural Center, Hawaii's most popular paid attraction. Next is Kahuku, an old plantation camp and gateway to the famed surfing beaches of the North Shore. The Sunset Beach and Waimea Bay surf spots are visible from the highway; the Banzai Pipeline is directly across from Sunset Beach Elementary School. Whether it's winter (when the surf is big and dangerous) or summer (when the swimming is superb), take a look at this world-famous stretch of sand.

Turn up the hill on Pupukea Road, then take the first right into Puu Mahuka Heiau, Oahu's largest place of pre-Christian worship. Perfect for quiet meditation, this ancient stone platform above the Pacific commands its scene like a Greek temple. Half a mile beyond Pupukea Road,

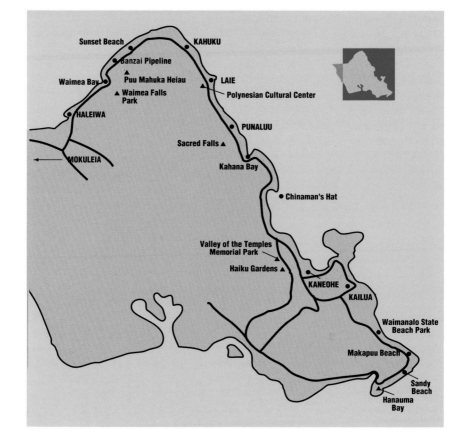

the highway takes a deep curve around Waimea Bay past Waimea Falls Park. Waimea Bay, like most North Shore spots, is excellent for swimming in summer and spectacular for surf-watching in winter.

Continue on to Haleiwa, where you just might be ready for dinner or perhaps a "shave ice." If you've made good time so far, consider driving on west to Mokuleia for its seaside polo fields, or to Dillingham Field for a glider ride.

The drive back to Honolulu on the H-2 and H-1 freeways (45 minutes to an hour and a half, depending on freeway traffic) traverses Oahu's agricultural central plain past the Dole Plantation Visitors Pavilion (a "must" stop for pineapple lovers), and skirts the sprawling military installations at Schofield Barracks, Wheeler Army Air Field, and Pearl Harbor.

1

2

3

1. *Waimanalo Beach*
2. *Makapuu Beach*
3. *Dole Cannery*
4. *Aerial view of Kailua*

2. THE NUUANU PALI AND THE WINDWARD BEACHES

A relatively short visit to the spectacular Nuuanu Pali and the public beaches at Kailua and Lanikai shows off Oahu's most famous views and two of its best beaches. From Waikiki, take the H-1 freeway westbound to the Pali Highway exit. Follow that busy route through cool Nuuanu Valley and the Koolau mountains.

A mile up Pali Highway, look for Queen Emma's Summer Palace on the right. The simple, gracious residence, set in a garden, includes a small museum displaying memorabilia of the unique Hawaiian-European lifestyle of Hawaii's royalty in the mid-nineteenth century.

As Pali Highway climbs, take the Nuuanu Pali Lookout exit to one of the most famous views in Hawaii. From the lookout high on the cliffs, Windward Oahu is spread out before you. The wind, funneled up the cliffsides, can be treacherous but fun. Nuuanu Pali was the scene of the bloody climax of the 1795 battle between Oahu's defenders and Kamehameha's invading army that led to the unification of the Hawaiian Kingdom.

Return to the Pali Highway and head through the tunnels toward Kailua. Continue past the small business section to Kailua Beach Park. Famed for wind-surfing, sparkling Kailua Bay with its long crescent beach is popular with families, canoe paddlers, kayakers, and sun worshipers, particularly early in the day. By late afternoon in normal trade-wind weather, the sun is behind the clouds that pile up against the mountains.

Lanikai, a lovely laid-back residential area past Kailua Beach Park, has one of Oahu's favorite (and least crowded) beaches, noted for its calm turquoise water and dazzling golden sand. Offshore are the picturesque twin Mokulua islands.

Return to Honolulu and Waikiki either by the same route or around the southeast corner of the island via Waimanalo and Makapuu Point.

1. Chinaman's Hat
2. Kailua Beach

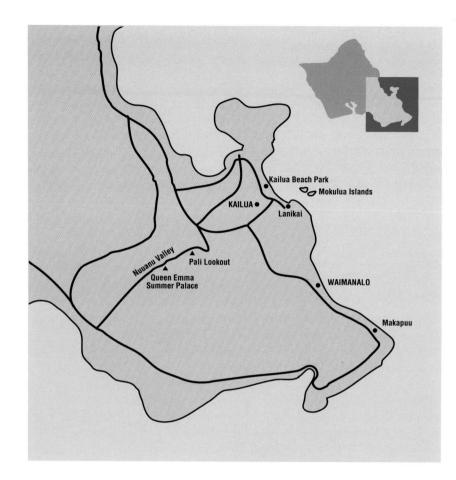

Kailua Beach Park

Mokulua Islands

KAILUA

Lanikai

Nuuanu Valley

▲ Pali Lookout

▲ Queen Emma
Summer Palace

WAIMANALO

Makapuu

3. View from the Pali lookout
4. Lanikai Beach

4

3. PEARL HARBOR/ARIZONA MEMORIAL/LEEWARD OAHU

From Waikiki, take the H-1 westward to the U.S.S. Arizona Memorial exit signs. The National Park Service visitor center at the Pearl Harbor Naval Base offers a free 20-minute film on the events of December 7, 1941, and a shuttle-boat ride to the offshore memorial structure.

Leaving Pearl Harbor, follow the signs to H-1 West and continue to the island's Leeward coast. This most rural part of Oahu, extending from Nanakuli up the coast to Maili, Waianae, and Makaha, faces big resort development. It has excellent swimming, snorkeling, and fishing (as well as great sunsets). Winter brings big surfing waves into Makaha and Yokohama Beaches near the end of the road. Return to Waikiki by the same route.

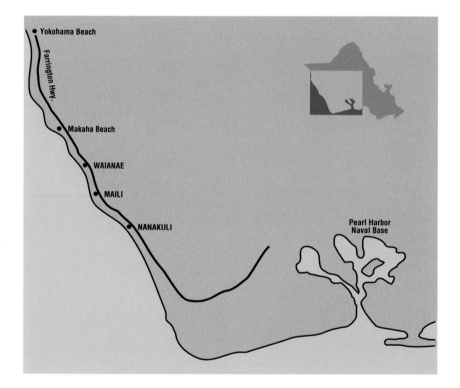

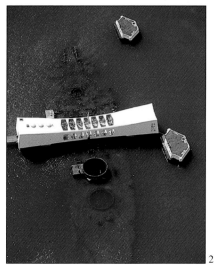

1. Pearl Harbor
2. Arizona Memorial
3. Yokohama Beach
4. Aerial of Pearl Harbor

4. HONOLULU PROPER

A walking tour of Honolulu's compact and attractive Downtown, easily accessible from Waikiki by a 15-minute bus ride (parking is scarce and expensive), covers Hawaii's corporate, banking, and government center, as well as giving glimpses of life in the early days.

Palm-lined Bishop Street, the "Wall Street of the Pacific," is Downtown's main thoroughfare. Sleek high-rises and elegant mission-style business houses create a unique architectural blend. Tanned men in muted-print aloha shirts and professional women wearing flowing muumuus with flower leis around their shoulders lend an unmistakably tropical feeling to America's newest and most exotic Downtown.

Two blocks east of Bishop Street is a handsomely gardened group of government buildings: Iolani Palace, the former seat of the monarchy (guided tours are available by appointment); the exuberant State Capitol; Aliiolani Hale judiciary building with its heroic statue of King Kamehameha; the California-style City Hall, Honolulu Hale; historic Washington Place, a nineteenth-century mansion now the official residence of Hawaii's governor; Kawaiahao Church, "Honolulu's Westminster Abbey," built in 1836; and the Mission Houses Museum next door.

Three blocks in the opposite direction is Chinatown, Honolulu's oldest intact urban neighborhood. Pre-World War II low-rise buildings house Chinese herbalists, flower shops, banks, Vietnamese restaurants, jade dealers, raffish bars, X-rated theaters, and chic art galleries. Don't miss Wo Fat, a busy Cantonese restaurant in a landmark Chinese-style building on Hotel Street, and Oahu Market, a pungent, open-air fish, produce, and flower emporium.

From this point, the capital's cultural attractions are widespread so a car is recommended. The most important include: the Bernice Pauahi Bishop Museum, the world's leading repository of Hawaiian and Polynesian cultural artifacts and natural history specimens; the Honolulu Academy of Arts with its collections of Asian, European, and American art, housed in an extremely handsome hybrid of native Hawaiian, Asian, and mission architectural styles; Hawaii Maritime Center at Honolulu Harbor with lively displays on Hawaii's economic and recreational ties to the sea; and The Contemporary Museum, with new collections of American, Asian, and local art in a lovely old hillside mansion.

Other points of interest are the Lyon Arboretum in Manoa Valley, Puu Ualakaa State Park in the hills above Honolulu (with a fantastic view of south Oahu), the National Cemetery of the Pacific in Punchbowl Crater and Diamond Head Crater, reached by a road tunnel.

You will find more information about all the foregoing in the Facts section that follows.

Rainbow

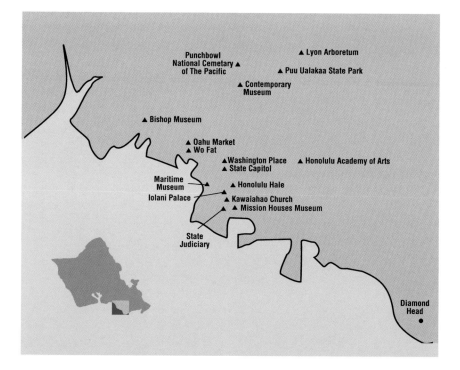

Punchbowl
National Cemetary ▲
of The Pacific

▲ Lyon Arboretum

▲ Puu Ualakaa State Park

▲ Contemporary
Museum

▲ Bishop Museum

▲ Oahu Market
▲ Wo Fat

▲Washington Place   ▲ Honolulu Academy of Arts
▲ State Capitol

Maritime
Museum   ▲ Honolulu Hale

Iolani Palace   ▲ Kawaiahao Church
▲ Mission Houses Museum

State
Judiciary

Diamond
Head

1. *Bishop Museum interior*
2. *600 ft. Chinese dragon*
3. *Lei*

143

OAHU FACTS

AIRPORT

See Honolulu International Airport

ALA MOANA BEACH PARK

Where locals go

Opposite the Ala Moana Shopping Center. Get there before 9 a.m. on weekends and holidays for convenient parking.

ALA MOANA CENTER

Hawaii's largest mall

When it opened in 1959, this 50-acre treat was the largest open-air shopping center in the world. With 180 stores and restaurants, including Hawaii's largest food court, 7,800 parking spaces, a post office and an entertainment stage, it is a unique must-visit experience. Stop and enjoy the free Young People's Hula Show every Sunday at 9:30 a.m

The center is open without charge Monday through Friday, 9:30 a.m. to 9 p.m.; Saturday and Sunday hours are a bit shorter. On Ala Moana Boulevard, ten to twenty minutes' walk from central Waikiki, the mall is also accessible by the No. 8 City Bus or by the Pineapple Transit from Waikiki for 50 cents.

ALOHA TOWER

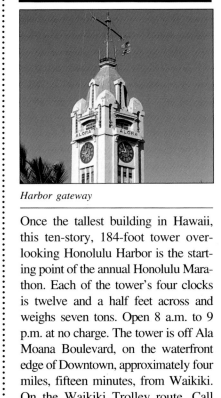

Harbor gateway

Once the tallest building in Hawaii, this ten-story, 184-foot tower overlooking Honolulu Harbor is the starting point of the annual Honolulu Marathon. Each of the tower's four clocks is twelve and a half feet across and weighs seven tons. Open 8 a.m. to 9 p.m. at no charge. The tower is off Ala Moana Boulevard, on the waterfront edge of Downtown, approximately four miles, fifteen minutes, from Waikiki. On the Waikiki Trolley route. Call 536-6801 for information.

AQUARIUM

See Waikiki Aquarium.

U.S.S. *ARIZONA* MEMORIAL

View of the memorial

This shrine, spanning the sunken battleship *Arizona*, honors the more than 1,500 who lost their lives on December 7, 1941, when the Japanese attacked Pearl Harbor, provoking the United States' entry in World War II. The National Park Service operates a visitor center with a free program that includes a 20-minute film about the Pearl Harbor attack and a shuttle-boat ride to the memorial. The program is not offered on Thanksgiving, Christmas, and New Year's Day.

Tickets are handed out on a first-come, first-served basis starting at 7:30 a.m. Because the demand to tour the memorial is great, waits are sometimes as long as two or three hours. Each person must obtain his own ticket. Shirts and footwear are required on the shuttle-boat ride, and children must be accompanied by an adult.

A visitor center museum and bookstore operated by the nonprofit Arizona Memorial Museum Association are open from 7:30 a.m. to 5 p.m. They may be contacted by calling 422-5905 or 422-5664. For recorded park information call 422-0561.

The World War II combat submarine *Bowfin* is moored nearby and is open to the public.

The Arizona Memorial is adjacent to the Ford Island ferry terminal off Kamehameha Highway 14 miles from Waikiki and can be reached by city bus (Route 20), by private car (although parking is limited), or commercial tour. The Arizona Memorial Shuttle Bus (phone 926-4747) costs $3 in each direction, $5 for the round trip. If you drive, take H-1 West past the airport to the Arizona Memorial/Stadium exit. Follow the signs approximately one and a half miles to the Arizona Memorial Visitor Center.

U.S. ARMY MUSEUM OF HAWAII

Highlights of the military history of Hawaii and the U.S. Army in Hawaii from the days of King Kamehameha are on display. Weapons, uniforms, and more are housed in a World War I coast artillery battery. Open daily except Monday, 10 a.m. to 4:30 p.m. No charge. Fort DeRussy, on Kalia Road, in Waikiki.

BEACHES

Sandy Beach

Oahu's beaches are perfect for swimming, camping, body-boarding, surfing, wind-surfing, canoeing kayaking, sailing, snorkeling, scuba diving, and just plain tanning. Water temperatures range from 75° to 80° Fahrenheit all year.

In Honolulu, Ala Moana Beach Park and familiar Waikiki Beach are ideal starters. Get there early; the best spots

Waimea Bay

on the sand fill quickly during weekends and holidays. To get away from the crowds, try less frequented Kaimana Beach, between the old Natatorium and the New Otani Hotel on Kalakaua Avenue near Diamond Head, or quiet Kaalawai Beach just beyond Diamond Head.

Going east around the island, Hanauma Bay Beach Park is famous for its snorkeling and swimming. Nearby Makapuu and Sandy Beach are the premier body-surfing beaches on Oahu. Sandy Beach is for experts only. Because it is in shallow water, the shore "break" is especially dangerous. Scene of the annual Gotcha Pro Surf Championships that consistently attract excellent athletes, surf conditions at "Sandy" range from good to awesome. Watch for the riptide and hang on to your swimsuit. About sixteen miles, 35 minutes, from Waikiki, past Hanauma Bay and the Blowhole, on Kalanianaole Highway. City buses pass twice an hour.

The Windward shore extends northward from Makapuu Point some forty miles to Kahuku Point, with many smaller and less famous beaches. Kailua Beach Park, Lanikai and Waimanalo Beach Parks are favorite swimming spots. Prevailing northeast trade winds provide good sailing and wind-surfing year round. Be careful of the blue "Portuguese man-of-war"—stinging

Lanikai

jellyfish that sometimes wash ashore during and after storms.

The North Shore beaches such as Waimea and Sunset are fine during the summer but, because they are unprotected by offshore reefs, they are dangerous from November through April. The outrageous winter surf is a threat to even expert swimmers. Stay well back from the water's edge during high surf periods. Be careful at any beach but especially at those between Kahuku and Mokuleia. The waves that roll in are often bigger than you think and can generate strong currents.

On the Leeward west shore from Kaena Point to Barbers Point, Makaha Beach is the most famous. The North Shore precautions also apply here.

BERNICE PAUAHI BISHOP MUSEUM

The world's finest collection of Hawaiian and Polynesian cultural artifacts and natural history specimens is at the Bishop Museum, established in 1889 as a memorial to Princess Bernice Pauahi Bishop by her husband, Charles Reed Bishop. It is a leading natural science and anthropological research institution. On the grounds are a planetarium, a 90,000-volume library, a gift shop, a small restaurant, a brand new exhibit building, and much more. There is a *hula* show every day at 1 p.m.

The museum, in the Kalihi district approximately 30 minutes from Waikiki, is open daily, 9 a.m. to 5 p.m. Admission for adults is $5.95; youths (six to 17), senior citizens and active military, $4.95; children under six, free. 1525 Bernice Street, Honolulu, Hawaii 96817. Call 847-3511 for information.

Natural science center

BLOWHOLE

The Halona Blowhole formed long ago when hot lava cooled on the outside while the molten interior continued to flow. Later, the sea broke a hole through the lava tube. Today, heavy surf pressurizes the air in the tube, forcing a jet of water and spray through the reef top. The Blowhole is on Kalanianaole Highway, past Hanauma Bay about thirty minutes from Waikiki.

BOWFIN SUBMARINE MUSEUM

This is your chance to see a real World War II combat submarine, the U.S.S. *Bowfin*. All eight below-deck compartments are open to visitors. Self-guided tours use hand-held radio receivers. Open 8 a.m. to 5 p.m., except Thanksgiving, Christmas, and New Year's. Six dollars for adults gets admission to the submarine and the adjacent Pacific Submarine Museum; $3 for retirees and active duty personnel with military ID; children, $1; uniformed personnel enter free. Children under six cannot board the submarine but are welcome in the Pacific Submarine Museum. Bowfin Park is adjacent to the U.S.S. *Arizona* Memorial Visitor Center. Call 423-1341.

BYODO-IN TEMPLE

Buddhist tribute

This replica of a 900-year-old Buddhist temple in Kyoto, Japan, was built in 1968 to honor Hawaii's first Japanese immigrants. It has a two-acre reflecting pond ablaze with multicolor carp, a three-ton bronze bell, and an 18-foot Buddha. Admission is free to the memorial park, open 8 a.m. to 4:30 p.m. The temple is at the Valley of the Temples Memorial Park, on Kahekili Highway past Kaneohe, approximately 45 minutes from Waikiki. Call 239-8811 for information.

CHILDREN'S MUSEUM OF ARTS, CULTURE, SCIENCE, & TECHNOLOGY

For anyone traveling with children this new establishment emphasizes fun interactive exhibits. Open Tuesday through Friday, 9 a.m. to 1 p.m.; Saturday and Sunday, 10 a.m. to 4 p.m. Admission charge. In Dole Cannery Square, 650 Iwilei Road, approximately five miles from Waikiki. Call 522-0040.

CHINAMAN'S HAT

Reptile isle

This aptly named conical island's Hawaiian name is Mokolii, "the little lizard." It is just offshore from Kualoa Point State Park on the Windward side, between Kahaluu and Kaaawa on your way to Laie, and about one hour from Waikiki.

CHINATOWN

Honolulu's Chinatown lies on the airport side of Downtown. Take the Pineapple Transit, or hop on the Waikiki Trolley and get off at Wo Fat Restaurant. It's always fascinating, but it really comes alive Saturday mornings.

Try some real back-home Asian cooking at one of the many mom-and-dad restaurants (check out the daily specials), or at venerable Wo Fat for reliably good Chinese food. Wander into fresh noodle factories, open Asian food markets, herbalist shops, small ethnic grocery and clothing shops, or River Street Market, all part of the unique charm and variety of the area. If you want a fresh lei, the flower stands on Maunakea Street are brilliant with color and offer some of the best deals in town. Peek into the Chinese Cultural Plaza on the mountain side of Beretania Street for another display of exotic food and merchandise.

You also may want to take either of the following walking tours for an entertaining and informative overview of the area:

•**Hawaii Heritage Center Chinatown Tour**. Every Friday (except holidays), 9:30 a.m. to 12:30 p.m. Admission charge. Go to 1128 Smith Street, 2nd floor, or call 521-2749.

•**Chinese Chamber of Commerce Walking Tour**. Every Tuesday. Admission charge for a three-hour tour. Call 533-3181.

Exotic goods and food

THE CONTEMPORARY MUSEUM

Gallery and cafe

This institution focuses on significant artists of the last four decades with both permanent and traveling exhibitions. Guided tours are available. A gift shop and cafe are on the premises. Open Tuesday through Saturday, 10 a.m. to 4 p.m.; Sunday 1 to 4 p.m. Introductory membership is $3 for adults, children under 15 are free. 2411 Makiki Heights Drive, uphill from Roosevelt High School.

DIAMOND HEAD

Lying dormant for approximately 150,000 years, this volcano is Hawaii's most distinctive landmark. There are no diamonds on Diamond Head. Sailors in the 1800s found calcite crystals that resembled diamonds, and the name stuck. Diamond Head is a State park where everyone is welcome.

Take the Diamond Head Crater Rim hike if you visit the park. The 0.7 mile trail from the crater floor climbs approximately 540 feet and includes a 99-step stairway. Paved at the bottom, the trail later is covered with rock and slippery gravel so a good pair of walking shoes is recommended. It's a brisk walk, but the view from the top is spectacular! Allow 60 minutes going up and 45 coming down. Stick to the trail!

Park hours are 6 a.m. to 6 p.m. From central Waikiki, find the entrance by heading toward Diamond Head, then at the Honolulu Zoo turn up Monsarrat Avenue and Diamond Head Road to the entrance arrow just past Kapiolani Community College. The No. 58 City Bus also takes you there.

The Clean Air Team conducts a hike at 9 a.m. on Saturdays. Meet at the colorful windsock in front of Honolulu Zoo and bring your flashlight. Donation is $3. Call 944-0804 for information.

A famous Hawaii landmark

DIAMOND HEAD LOOKOUT

A windsurfer's dream

As you drive around the ocean side of Diamond Head toward Hanauma Bay from Waikiki, look for this popular turnoff just past the lighthouse. You get not only a great view but an opportunity to see some excellent surfers and wind-surfers, plus occasional whales, warships and yachts.

149

DINING

If you like to eat, Honolulu is for you. Cuisines? "American," Chinese, Continental, Filipino, French, Hawaiian, Italian, Japanese, Korean, Thai . . . It's here. Try a local plate lunch, available at any lunch wagon or drive-in. And for dessert, a *malasada*, a piece of *haupia* pudding, or a slice of macadamia nut pie.

Tip: Don't be afraid to venture out of Waikiki! The city is full of excellent eating places. The Makai Marketplace at Ala Moana Shopping Center, only a mile away, has an unbelievable range of foods. Nearby, Ward Warehouse and Ward Centre (also on Ala Moana Boulevard) likewise offer excellent restaurants and fast-food shops. All are within walking distance of Waikiki, but you can get to these places on the No. 19 or No. 20 City Bus, by cab, or on the Waikiki Trolley. Further down Ala Moana Boulevard is Restaurant Row, with eating places, discos and shopping.

Toward Diamond Head from Waikiki is Kapahulu Avenue. Walk inland from the ocean, past the public library and the Ala Wai golf course. You will find at least seventeen medium-price ethnic restaurants as well as fast food places. Just choose one and walk in.

Only minutes from Waikiki, Kapiolani Boulevard and Keeaumoku Street are also heavily laden with ethnic restaurants, particularly Korean and Japanese. Cruise along either street and select the most inviting. Happy eating!

DIVING AND SNORKELING

Swim with the fishes

You might consider going to Waikiki Aquarium first—before you get wet. But if you're anxious to start, Hanauma Bay is a good place. Get there early for parking, and do not leave valuables in your car. Several companies companies specialize in half- and full-day Hanauma Bay snorkeling tours. They offer hotel pickup service, snorkeling equipment and fishfood. Underwater cameras and masks with corrective lens are also available. Both city and private buses offer regular service from Waikiki to Hanauma Bay.

If you are new to scuba diving in Hawaii you may want to contact one of the dive shops that offer snorkeling and scuba instruction. Diving here has its own character, about which you should inform yourself.

Scuba tours range in price from about $40 to $60. They usually include instruction for beginners and are closely supervised.

DOLE CANNERY SQUARE

Marked by the 195-foot Dole pineapple, the 100,000-gallon heart of the cannery's fire protection system, Cannery Square features shops, cafes, exhibits, and murals and is open free to the public. Tours of the cannery run continuously for a $5 fee. Children 12 and under are free when accompanied by an adult.

The square is open daily, 9 a.m. to 5 p.m. 650 Iwilei Road, approximately fifteen minutes from central Waikiki. Call 531-8855 for information.

Free bus service from selected Waikiki hotels is provided by Dole Cannery. A free Hilo Hattie bus will take you to the square from the Kodak Hula Show every Tuesday, Wednesday, and Thursday. There is a 50 cent charge on the Pineapple Transit.

DOLE PINEAPPLE PAVILION

Fruit and juice oasis

On your way to the North Shore via Route 99, look for a grove of eucalyptus trees rising from an ocean of pineapples about 3 miles past Wahiawa. Fresh-cut pineapple, juice, ice-cold Dole Whip, and Dole souvenirs await you. Open 9 a.m. to 5:30 p.m. No admission charge. On Kamehameha Highway, approximately 28 miles from Waikiki via H-1 and H-2, through Wahiawa. Call 621-8408 for information.

DOWNTOWN HONOLULU

A magical history tour

Within a two-mile radius of Iolani Palace are a dozen or more places to see— a great setup for productive walking. The simplest way to reach Downtown is on the Waikiki Trolley or the No. 2 City Bus. Get off at the State Capitol and have your camera handy.

On the mountain side of the capitol is the Father Damien memorial statue. Across Beretania Street is the Eternal Flame monument. Adjacent to the north is Washington Place (the governor's official residence) and Saint Andrew's Cathedral. Head back to the capitol and this time go toward the ocean, where a statue of Queen Liliuokalani greets you. Continue across the courtyard to Iolani Palace Grounds.

Tip: Go to the Palace Bandstand at noon on Friday for a free Royal Hawaiian Band concert. Bring a sandwich and enjoy.

Directly across King Street from Iolani Palace is Aliiolani Hale State Judiciary building and the King Kamehameha statue. Walk toward Diamond Head on King Street across Punchbowl Street to Kawaiahao Church and the adjoining Mission Houses Museum. Seek out the Hawaiian Heritage Museum next door for an excellent selection of Hawaiian books and crafts. Finally, retrace your steps up Punchbowl Street to the capitol and continue westward on Beretania Street.

Honolulu, viewed from the waterfront

Another exploring suggestion is to check out Chinatown first, ending on River Street. Look around River Street Market, then head inland. Your walk will take you past the Chinese Cultural Plaza, where you can shop and get a tasty lunch. Continuing up Nuuanu Stream, cross Vineyard Boulevard and enter Foster Botanic Garden. Relax a while in this lush green park full of rare and interesting plants.

The Waikiki Trolley stops in Chinatown, at the Honolulu Academy of Arts at Thomas Square, and at Aloha Tower and *Falls of Clyde.*

DUKE PAOA KAHANAMOKU

Surfing and swimming champ

At the edge of the surf at Waikiki is a statue honoring Hawaii's famous and beloved Duke Paoa Kahanamoku. (Duke was his given name, not a title.) Born on Maui in 1890, this Hawaiian athlete developed a swimming style he called "the Hawaiian crawl."

Using it as a member of the U.S. team at the 1912 Olympic Games in Stockholm, he smashed the world record for the 100-meter sprint. As "the American crawl," it became a basic competition stroke everywhere.

Kahanamoku is widely known for his success in promoting surfboarding, a sport once reserved exclusively for Hawaiian royalty. The Duke Kahanamoku Invitational Surfing Championship Meet each winter on Oahu's North Shore, as well as other events and activities, commemorate this gracious and talented man.

EAST-WEST CENTER JAPANESE GARDEN

Tranquil landscape

Tucked in a corner of the University of Hawaii's main campus in Manoa Valley, this quietly elegant garden at the East-West Center is an oasis of peace and tranquility. There is no admission fee, but you must pay for campus parking. Use the Dole Street entrance to the university, the one closest to Saint Louis Heights. Park past the sign that says "East-West Center." The garden behind Jefferson Hall is open daily. There is a free tour of the East-West Center and the garden every Wednesday at 1:30 p.m. Meet at Jefferson Hall in the Friends Lounge, Garden Level. Fifteen minutes from Waikiki.

ETERNAL FLAME

A beacon of hope

Across Beretania Street from the State Capitol, the Eternal Flame burns as a tribute to the men and women of Hawaii who served in the U.S. armed services, and as "a beacon of courage and hope for all mankind." The Waikiki Trolley stops directly across the street.

FALLS OF CLYDE

Tall-masted masterpiece

This beautifully restored four-masted iron-hull sailing ship, the last of its kind in the world, is now part of the Hawaii Maritime Center. Built in Scotland more than a century ago, it sailed regularly from San Francisco to Hawaii as one of the first vessels of today's Matson Line. Open 9 a.m.

to 5 p.m. Admission to the center: adults, $7; children six to 17, $4; five and under, free. Pier 7, where *Falls of Clyde* is moored, is a stone's throw from Aloha Tower (Pier 9), about four miles from Waikiki. Call 536-6373 for museum information.

Tip: There is a small restaurant at the end of the museum pier, with a great view of harbor activity.

FATHER DAMIEN MEMORIAL STATUE

Remembering Molokai's martyr

The first documented case of leprosy appeared in Hawaii in 1835. A Belgian priest, Father Joseph Damien de Veuster, dedicated his life to serving at the leprosy colony (today's Kalaupapa settlement) established in 1866 on Molokai's remote Kalawao Peninsula. Remembered as the Martyr of Molokai, this compassionate and religious man lived, worked, and in 1889 died of the disease among the lepers.

The statue of Father Damien created by artist Marisol Escobar stands in front of the State Capitol in downtown Honolulu. To view the statue take the Waikiki Trolley or No. 2 City Bus to the capitol.

FATHER DAMIEN
MUSEUM AND ARCHIVES

Museum in his honor

Houses photographs, films, and the personal effects of Father Damien. Open Monday through Friday, 9 a.m. to 3 p.m.; Saturday, 9 a.m. to noon. No admission charge. 130 Ohua Street, at the Diamond Head end of Waikiki, two streets before the Honolulu Zoo. Call 923-2690.

SENATOR FONG'S
PLANTATION AND GARDENS

Senatorial scenery

This 725-acre plantation features more that 75 varieties of edible fruits and nuts, lush tropical forests, natural scenery, landscaped gardens of exotic flowers, and panoramic views of Windward Oahu, the majestic Koolau Mountains, and historic Kaneohe Bay. Special gardens honor the five presidents that Senator Fong served during his

seventeen years in the U.S. Senate. Guided open-air tram tours, lei-making classes, tropical fruits, snacks, lunches, and unique gifts are available.

Open 10 a.m. to 4 p.m. Adult admission, $6.50; juniors, $3; children five and under, free. Heading toward Laie on Kamehameha Highway, watch for road signs three miles past the Valley of Temples. Nineteen miles from Waikiki. Phone 239-6775.

FOSTER BOTANIC GARDENS

Downtown retreat

William Hillebrand, a physician and botanist, started importing plants to Hawaii during the reign of King Kamehameha III. He introduced many plants, especially trees, to the islands before selling his home and gardens to Captain and Mrs. Thomas Foster in 1867. The Fosters enlarged the garden, adding trees and flowers, and bequeathed their property to Honolulu in 1930.

This 20-acre showcase of Hawaii's rare trees, shrubs, and flowers contains 24 of the more than a hundred individual trees designated as "exceptional" on Oahu. The Lyon Orchid Garden is on the grounds.

Open 9 a.m. to 4 p.m. Admission for adults is $1; children under 12, free when with an adult. Guided tours on Monday, Tuesday, and Wednesday. On North Vineyard Boulevard, inland of downtown Honolulu, 25 minutes from Waikiki by car. Call 531-1939 for information.

HAIKU GARDENS

Windward Eden

This beautiful, quiet garden is popular for weddings. The grounds include a water lily pond and an excellent restaurant. No admission charge for the garden. Located on Haiku Road, in Kaneohe, fourteen miles, approximately 25 minutes, from Waikiki. Call 637-8005 for information on the restaurant.

HALEIWA

This once-sleepy North Shore community is known primarily for its excellent winter surf and for Matsumoto Store's "shave ice." The rustic charm of Haleiwa, "house of the frigate bird," is still evident, although its roadside stands and hand-painted signs must now compete with chain restaurants and surf shops. You can still sample the laid-back lifestyle of Hawaii, however, when you stop and watch the people. About 45 minutes from Waikiki, via H-1 and H-2, nine miles past Wahiawa on Route 83.

HANAUMA BAY

This 101-acre State underwater park is a great place to swim, snorkel, dive or just people-watch. In an eroded ancient volcanic crater, Hanauma Bay's crystal water teems with some of the nosiest reef fish around. Take a bag of frozen green peas for feeding the fish (but be sure to dispose of the bag on shore). Go early to get good parking, and do not leave valuables in your car. This is a State Marine Life Conservation District; you cannot "fish for, catch, take, injure, kill, possess, or remove any marine life."

Off Kalanianaole Highway (Route 72) between Hawaii Kai and Sea Life Park, Hanauma Bay is twelve miles from Waikiki, and you can get there on the No. 58 City Bus. A special No. 22 Beach Bus leaves Honolulu Zoo every hour starting at 9:05 a.m.; the last bus leaves at 4:05 p.m.

Half-sunken crater

HAWAII KAI

Hawaii Kai, a residential community eastward past Aina Haina and Niu Valley, was the brainchild of the late billionaire industrialist Henry J. Kaiser, who developed an expanse of *kiawe* (mesquite) flatland and a shallow fishpond into an affluent suburb. Wanting to live close to his dream, he built a mansion, with guest houses, pools, boathouse and dock, tennis courts, and an air-conditioned kennel for his poodles. The entire Kaiser estate was painted in his wife's favorite flamingo pink. You'll pass Hawaii Kai on Kalanianaole Highway as you head east toward Hanauma Bay. (photo on next page).

Hawaii Kai

HAWAII MARITIME CENTER

Sitting in the shadow of Aloha Tower at the harbor end of Bishop Street, this two-floor museum contains everything pertinent to Hawaii's maritime history. Open 9 a.m. to 5 p.m. Admission for adults is $7; children six to seventeen, $4; up to six, free. On Pier 7 off Ala Moana Boulevard, approximately 15 minutes from Waikiki. Call 536-6373. There is a good restaurant and bar at the end of the pier, a reserved seat for watching harbor activity.

HICKAM AIR FORCE BASE

Named for Lieutenant Colonel Horace Meek Hickam and activated in 1938, Hickam AFB is headquarters for Pacific Air Forces (PACAF), a major air command and air component of the U.S. Pacific Command responsible for the defense of more than a hundred million square miles. Situated between Pearl Harbor and Honolulu International Airport, Hickam AFB encompasses more than 2,700 acres of working and living space for its 6,130 military and 2,169 civilian personnel. It is nine miles from downtown Honolulu, twelve miles from Waikiki.

HONOLULU ACADEMY OF ARTS

International collections

The Honolulu Academy of Arts houses world-respected collections of Oriental, European, and American art. Forty-five-minute tours every Tuesday, Wednesday, Friday and Saturday start at 11 a.m.; Thursday at 2 p.m.; and Sunday at 1 p.m. Galleries are open Tuesday through Saturday, 10 a.m. to 4:30 p.m.; Sunday, 1 to 5 p.m. Free. Downtown, at 900 South Beretania Street, approximately three miles from Waikiki. On the Waikiki Trolley route or by City Bus No. 2. Call 538-1006 or 538-3693.

HONOLULU HARBOR

Home to freighters and luxury liners

Once known as Kou ("sheltered bay"), Honolulu Harbor was responsible for turning the port into the largest and most important city in the central Pacific. Although Kaneohe Bay is comparable in depth and size, winds on the Honolulu side are more favorable. Pearl Harbor, protected from storms, long was inaccessible because of reefs at the entrance. Despite recent declines in shipping, 13.8 million tons of cargo and 87,221 passengers passed through Honolulu Harbor as recently as 1991.

HONOLULU INTERNATIONAL AIRPORT

Central Pacific hub

With more than 34 trans-Pacific and inter-island airlines, Honolulu International Airport—approximately nine miles from Waikiki (allow 30 minutes transit time)—served over 11.8 million passengers in 1990.

If you have luggage and have not prearranged your pickup, a cab (about $15 during rush hours) or one of the following shuttle services will take you directly to and from your Waikiki hotel:

• *Airport Express.* 6 a.m. to 10 p.m. Adults, $5; children , $2.50. Call 949-5249 for schedules.

• *Airport Motorcoach.* 6:30 a.m. to 10 p.m. Adults, $5; children, $2.50. Call 926-4747.

HONOLULU STAKE MORMON TABERNACLE

This historic building has been the center of the Church of Jesus Christ of Latter-day Saints' activities in the Islands since its dedication in August 1941. Nearby is a monument to the first Mormon missionaries who arrived in 1850. The large outdoor color mosaic of Jesus is a familiar landmark. Visitors are welcome.

The gardens include rare trees such as the Chinese banyan in front and the Loong Ngan tree shading the inner patio. Where Kalakaua Avenue intersects Beretania Street, three miles from Waikiki.

Monument to missionaries

HONOLULU ZOO

Waikiki bestiary

More than 800,000 visitors a year come to see animals from all over the world. Some are unique to Hawaii such as the endangered nene, the State bird. Check out the bird show, the children's petting zoo, and "The Wildest Show in Town," a free concert by local entertainers, every Wednesday evening during the summer. Bring a mat and your picnic dinner.

The zoo is open 8:30 a.m. to 4 p.m. Admission for adults is $3; children under 12, free when accompanying an adult. Walk toward Diamond Head on Kalakaua Avenue; you'll find the zoo at the intersection with Kapahulu Avenue. Call 971-7171 for information.

HOOMALUHIA BOTANIC GARDEN

Tropical greenery

Public, free. Four hundred acres of tropical trees and plants. Open 9 a.m. to 4 p.m. Closed Christmas and New Year's. At the end of Luluku Road in Ķaneohe. Call 235-6636 for information.

INTERNATIONAL MARKET PLACE

Bazaar beneath a banyan

With more than a hundred restaurants, shops, and kiosks, this unique open-air shopping area has the variety and color of an oriental bazaar shaded by glorious banyan trees. The International Food Court has 15 different menus to choose from. Open 9 a.m. to 11 p.m. No admission charge. 2330 Kalakaua Avenue, in the heart of Waikiki.

IOLANI PALACE AND GROUNDS

Downtown at King and Richards Streets, fifteen minutes from Waikiki. On the Waikiki Trolley route and the No. 2 City Bus.

Iolani Palace. The *Iolani*, "bird of heaven," was a symbol of Hawaiian royalty and a fitting name for the only formal royal palace in the United States. Iolani Palace recently has been beautifully restored after nine years and almost six million dollars. It was home to King David Kalakaua and Queen Liliuokalani during the twilight years of the Hawaiian monarchy that was overthrown in 1893.

Open for tours by reservation only, starting every fifteen minutes on Wednesday, Thursday, Friday, and Saturday from 9 a.m. to 2:15 p.m. Admission for adults is $4; children five to 12, $1. Children under five years are not permitted on this tour. For tour information call 538-1471. Reservations taken weekdays from 8 a.m. to 3:30 p.m. (522-0832).

Iolani Bandstand. This crown-shape structure was built in 1883 for the coronation of King Kalakaua and Queen Kapiolani. It is now the scene of gubernatorial inaugurations and public ceremonies, as well as Friday noon concerts by the Royal Hawaiian Band.

Iolani Barracks. Built in 1870 and originally sited several blocks away, this miniature fortress was once the headquarters and barracks of the Royal Household Guards.

Home of the monarchy

Iolani Bandstand

JOGGING

Footloose & fancy free

Brisk breezes and great scenery help to make Honolulu a jogger's paradise. Kapiolani Park, Ala Moana Park, and the Kahala area are popular choices.

KAENA POINT

The farthest point west on Oahu, Kaena, "the heat," is barren and desolate, no longer accessible even to four-wheel-drive vehicles. One of the State's best examples of coastal lowland and dune ecosystems, it was made a natural area reserve in 1983. Walk past the road's end, just beyond Mokuleia on Farrington Highway, at the far western end of Oahu's North Shore; or from the parking area at the bitter end of the Farrington Highway (route 930) from the other side on the Leeward coast.

Kaena Point

KAHALA

East of Diamond Head

With the famous Kahala Hilton Hotel and the exclusive Waialae Country Club as anchors, Kahala today is arguably Honolulu's most prestigious residential address. Half a century ago, the area was swampy farmland with a fringe of beach cottages along the shore.

KAHUKU SUGAR MILL

When cane was king

The Kahuku Plantation opened in 1890, when sugar was Hawaii's largest single source of income. In 1971 its relatively small, unreliable water supply and changes in the State's economy caught up with it. Three of the century-old mill's original steam engines, one dating from the Civil War, are in working condition. Tour the mill free, 8 a.m. to 9 p.m.

Surrounding the mill is a shopping complex featuring the Mill Restaurant (open 8 a.m. to 9 p.m.) and gift shops. Look for the tall red smokestack when you reach Kahuku, about forty miles (90 minutes) from Waikiki, past Laie and the Polynesian Cultural Center. Call 293-2414.

KAILUA

World-class wind-surfiing

Note 1,643-foot Mount Olomana at your right as you descend from the Nuuanu Pali to this populous Windward community at the end of Pali Highway. You'll also find Kailua Beach Park, thirty acres of first-rate beach and the best wind-surfing spot on Oahu. The flat island offshore is a bird sanctuary.

KAIMUKI

Old meets new

Kaimuki community, behind Diamond Head at the foot of Maunalani Heights, is a wonderful place for a small walking tour into the past. Park at the municipal lot off 12th and Harding Avenues. Inspect one of the neighborhood "crack seed stores" seemingly left over from the old days. Old and new restaurants sit side by side. Virtually all serve excellent food at reasonable prices.

KANEOHE

Suburb by the bay

Kaneohe, a large Windward residential suburb, includes the Marine Corps Air Station (see below) and the University of Hawaii Marine Biology Laboratory on Coconut Island. The Byodo-In Temple at the Valley of the Temples Memorial Park is another Kaneohe attraction. Follow the Likelike Highway exit from H-1 across the Koolaus, 35 minutes from Waikiki.

KANEOHE MARINE CORPS AIR STATION

The Corps on parade

Hawaii's central Pacific location makes it ideal for strategic deployment to the Far East, South Pacific and Indian Ocean. As part of the Fleet Marine Force-Pacific, more than 15,000 Marines, sailors, and their families are stationed on Mokapu Peninsula, at the edge of a Kaneohe Bay. The First Marine Expeditionary Brigade, an always-ready air-ground combat team stationed at Kaneohe, was one of the first units deployed to Saudi Arabia in Operation Desert Shield.

KAPIOLANI PARK

A popular park featuring a jogging track; large, open fields for kite flying, cricket, soccer, rugby, and baseball; an archery range; and tennis courts (usually crowded). Dedicated in 1877, it was Hawaii's first large public park. The annual Honolulu Marathon finishes in the park. A five-minute walk from central Waikiki, at the Diamond Head end of Kalakaua Avenue. Parking may be difficult on weekends and holidays, so try to get there before 9 a.m. The Honolulu Zoo, and the Waikiki Aquarium are nearby.

KAWAIAHAO CHURCH

Hawaii's 'Westminster'

Built in 1820 of nearly 14 thousand coral blocks, this is Honolulu's oldest and most famous church, with a mainly Hawaiian congregation. It is open from 8 a.m. to 4 p.m. Docents are on hand to help, Monday through Saturday from 9 a.m. to 3:30 p.m. Visitors are welcome at Sunday services (10:30 a.m.). A tour follows. On Punchbowl Street, a half block from the King Kamehameha statue, fifteen minutes from Waikiki. Call 522-1333

KING KAMEHAMEHA STATUE

The great unifier

This larger-than-life figure of Kamehameha the Great, unifier of the Hawaiian Islands, is actually the second casting done by American sculptor Thomas R. Gould. The original is on the Big Island. Located on the Waikiki Trolley route, outside the State judiciary building across from Iolani Palace, four miles from Waikiki.

KODAK HULA SHOW

This has been around more than 50 years and should not be missed! It not only features great singing and dancing, but is fun as well. Bright colors abound. Bring your camera and plenty of color film, but save some exposures for after the show when the performers will pose with you. Come early for the best seats. Performances every Tuesday, Wednesday, and Thursday at 10 a.m. Admission is $2.50. Located at the Waikiki Shell in Kapiolani Park, a half mile from central Waikiki. Walk down Kalakaua Avenue toward Diamond Head. Follow the crowd past the Honolulu Zoo on Monsarrat Avenue.

A free Hilo Hattie Bus runs to the Kodak Hula Show from selected Waikiki hotels. You can re-board after after the show for free transportation to the Hilo Hattie Clothing Factory and Dole Cannery Square. Call 537-2926 for information.

KOKO CRATER

Drought resisters

This old 1,208-foot tuff cone at the east end of Oahu is almost directly inland from Hanauma Bay on Kalanianaole Highway, 30 minutes from Waikiki. Inside the crater is an excellent botanical garden featuring drought-tolerant plants.

KOOLAU RANGE

Volcanic mountains

Stretching from Makapuu to Kahuku, the Koolau (windward) range is younger and larger than the leeward Waianae range, and forms the east half of Oahu island. Puu Konahuanui (3,150 feet), overlooking the North Shore, is its highest peak. Formed by volcanoes 2,200,000 to 2,500,000 years ago, the Koolaus separate the central Schofield plateau from rainy Windward Oahu.

LAIE

A predominantly Mormon community, Laie's cultural attractions include the Mormon Temple, the Hawaii campus of Brigham Young University, and the Polynesian Cultural Center (listed separately).

While in Laie, take your camera and check out the view from Laie Point. Go toward the water from Kamehameha Highway onto Anemoku Street. Then turn right and follow Naupaka Street to its end. Laie is at the opposite end of Oahu from Waikiki, roughly thirty-eight miles. Driving time is around ninety minutes.

LANIKAI

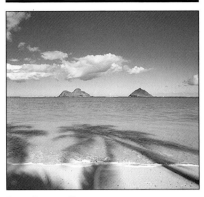

Sea of tranquility

An ancient fishing spot and later the site of watermelon farms, this comfortable Windward neighborhood between Kailua Bay and Waimanalo Bay has a mile of calm water that is great for swimming.

LYON ARBORETUM

Covering 124 acres in upper Manoa Valley, the Harold L. Lyon Arboretum is a research unit of the University of Hawaii. Facilities include greenhouses, a nursery, administrative and instruction buildings, an herbarium, reference materials, and specimens of many native and exotic plants. Guided tours start at 1 p.m. on the first Friday and third Wednesday of the month, and at 10 a.m. on the third Saturday. The arboretum is open Monday through Friday, 9 a.m. to 3 p.m.; Saturday, 9 a.m. to noon. Donation is $1.

Drive or take a city bus to the upper end of Manoa Road (don't confuse it with East Manoa Road), past Paradise Park, six miles from central Waikiki. Call 988-7378.

MAKIKI HEIGHTS

This attractive hillside neighborhood close to Downtown, bracketed by Tantalus ridge and Punchbowl Crater, is the home of many old-time Honolulu families.

MANOA

Cool, if cloudy, comfort

Manoa Valley, between Tantalus ridge and Saint Louis Heights, is a prestigious but comfortable residential area. From the University of Hawaii at its mouth to Paradise Park and Lyon Arboretum at its back, the valley is always cool, green and—in popular belief—rainy.

MISSION HOUSES MUSEUM

Three historic structures built between 1821 and 1841 are on display at the Mission Houses Museum. The white frame house, pre-cut in New England, brought around the Horn and erected on the site in 1821, was the first western-style home in Hawaii. The coral-block Chamberlain House, built in 1831, was the home, office, and depository for Levi Chamberlain, secular agent for the early Protestant missionaries. In the bedroom extension completed in 1841 is a replica of the old Ramage press used for the first Hawaiian language publications. Admission includes a 45-minute tour. A "Living History" program of costumed actors depicting people of Honolulu circa 1831 is offered every Saturday.

The museum is open Tuesday through Saturday, 9 a.m. to 4 p.m.; Sundays noon to 4 p.m.; closed Monday. Admission charge. Downtown at 553 South King Street, adjacent to Kawaiahao Church, four miles from Waikiki. On the Waikiki Trolley route. Call 531-0481.

A living legacy

MOANALUA GARDENS

Under the monkeypod

Spacious, beautifully shaped private park with large monkeypod and other tropical trees. Free, 23 acres. Off Puuloa and Moanalua roads on Route 78. Call 839-5334.

MOILIILI

Walking tour headquarters

Downhill from the University of Hawaii at the foot of Manoa Valley and ideal for a small walking tour, the Moiliili district is where old Honolulu mixes with the new. Pizza parlors stand next to open-air flower stores; a *hula* supply shop shares the sunshine with moderately priced ethnic restaurants, student bookstores and a softball diamond. When you are tired of walking, grassy Stadium Park is a great place to take it easy while others do the exercising.

MORMON TEMPLE, LAIE

Windward landmark

Members of the Church of Jesus Christ of Latter-day Saints make up about 85 percent of the Laie community, where this handsome white structure set in beautifully landscaped grounds offers a spectacular vista to the sea. You are welcome to tour the grounds and the adjacent visitor center. Laie is on Kamehameha Highway, about forty miles (90 to 110 minutes) from Waikiki.

NATIONAL MEMORIAL CEMETERY OF THE PACIFIC

Hallowed hill

Puowaina, "hill of sacrifice," the 114-acre National Memorial Cemetery of the Pacific situated in Punchbowl Crater, opened in 1949 as the final resting place for some 33,000 veterans and their dependents.

The 30-foot statue overlooking the rows of graves represents Columbia, as a symbol of all grieving mothers. On the marble walls leading up to the memorial building are the names of 28,745 servicemen missing in .action from World War II, Korea, and Vietnam. At the top of the stairs, several fascinating mosaic maps detail famous Pacific battles of the past half century. Open to visitors every day of the year: September 30-March 1, 8 a.m. to 5:30 p.m.; March 2-September 29, 8 a.m. to 6:30 p.m.; Memorial Day, 7 a.m. to 7 p.m. No charge. Follow the signs from downtown Honolulu, about twenty minutes from Waikiki.

NORTH SHORE

Haleiwa

Peaceful and placid in summer, with clear water and usually calm, sun-drenched bays, the North Shore of Oahu from Kahuku to Kaena Point is ideal for family picnics, swimming, and snorkeling. In winter, watch out! Storms thousands of miles away generate 20 to 25 foot waves that pound Waimea Bay, the Banzai Pipeline, and Sunset Beach without mercy and attract professional-level surfers from all over the world. Always check with the city lifeguard before going into the water on the North Shore, regardless of the season; there can be tricky riptides. Forty miles from Waikiki via H-1 and H-2, through Wahiawa and Haleiwa.

NUUANU PALI

Panorama nonpareil

On this historic site Kamehameha the Great's invading forces in April 1795 supposedly drove the Oahu defenders over the thousand-foot precipice, winning the Battle of Nuuanu and unifying the Hawaiian Islands. The Pali Lookout offers an unparalleled view of Windward Oahu, so bring your camera.

The Pali is fun on windy days. Go down the ramp on your right as you face the coastline. You can "fly" in the wind by leaning into it with your arms outstretched; watch residents show their visiting friends "how to." Ten miles from Waikiki, via Pali Highway.

Pali Lookout

NUUANU VALLEY

Nuuanu means "cool height." Early western arrivals chose this comfortable valley first for a summer retreat and later to build their homes. They planted many lush trees—monkeypods, African tulips, eucalyptus, and banyans—as well as the ferns and ginger that line the road. Nuuanu is seven miles, about twenty minutes, from Waikiki via Pali Highway. Look for the "Nuuanu Pali Drive" sign as you head up the hill; it's a detour worth taking.

Retreat from the heat

(MOUNT) OLOMANA See Kailua.

PACIFIC WHALING MUSEUM

Whaling artifacts, scrimshaw work, photographs and tools, with a sperm whale skeleton overhead. Daily lectures. A reference collection is available. Open 9:30 a.m. to 4:30 p.m.; Thursday, Friday, and Sunday evenings until 9:30. Free admission. On the grounds of Sea Life Park, at Makapuu Point. Call 259-7933.

PEARL HARBOR

Pearl Harbor Naval Base

Named for the oysters once harvested there, Pearl Harbor is the largest natural harbor in Hawaii. It was not a practical port, however, until 1898 when the coral reef blocking its entrance was finally dredged, permitting construction of dry docks, machine shops, training facilities, hospitals and capital ship anchorages. The name became famous when the Japanese on December 7, 1941, attacked the U.S. Navy ships based there, bringing the United States into World War II. A national historical landmark since 1965, it is the only naval base in the United States to be so designated.

The Pearl Harbor disaster ranks as one of the major events in American and Hawaiian history. Controversy remains as to why our forces were caught so completely by surprise in spite of numerous indications that trouble with Japan was imminent. Even the Imperial Japanese Admiralty had hardly expected such a complete destruction of America's naval power in the Pacific. In one hour and fifty minutes the attacking carrier-based planes managed to destroy virtually the entire American Pacific Fleet.

War and remembrance

Pearl Harbor Naval Base is the headquarters and nerve center of the U.S. Pacific Fleet, the world's largest naval command. The fleet includes more than 200 ships, 2,600 aircraft, and more than 250,000 Navy, Marine Corps and Coast Guard personnel. The command area covers 102 million square miles, stretching from the Arctic to the Antarctic, from the U.S. West Coast to the coast of East Africa.

You can get to Pearl Harbor, fourteen miles from Waikiki, via either H-1 West or Kamehameha Highway (Route 99). A pass is required to enter the base proper. Call 471-7110 for information.

PICNICKING

Just about any park or beach is open for picnics.

POLYNESIAN CULTURAL CENTER

This 42-acre slice of Polynesia operated by the Mormon Church offers tours, spectacular stage shows, and a "native" meal. Its main show and seven different Polynesian villages—the Marquesas, Hawaii, Fiji, Samoa, Tonga, Maori (New Zealand), and Tahiti—are actually hosted by young students from those islands.

Set aside the whole day to visit the center. The drive to Laie from Waikiki takes an hour and a half; exploring the villages and taking in the afternoon show finishes the day. Allow extra time if you stay for dinner and the evening show.

Open Monday through Saturday from 12:30 p.m., closed Sundays. For information, admission prices, and reservations, contact the Waikiki ticket office in the Royal Hawaiian Shopping Center on Kalakaua Avenue (Tel. 923-1861). The Polynesian Cultural Center is on Kamehameha Highway in Laie. Call 293-3333.

Cultural extravaganza

PUNCHBOWL

See National Cemetery of the Pacific.

PUU UALAKAA STATE PARK

Spectacular view

Drive up Tantalus via Round Top Drive for an unrivaled view from past Diamond Head to Pearl Harbor and beyond! Open 7:45 a.m. to 6:45 p.m.

QUEEN EMMA'S SUMMER PALACE

'Moon child'

This gracious old home in upper Nuuanu, looking out on Honolulu Harbor, was both retreat and social center for King Kamehameha IV, Queen Emma, and the royal family until the queen's death. They named it *Hanaiaka-malama* ("foster child of the moon") for a favorite Hawaiian demi-goddess. Purchased by the Hawaiian government as a public park, the palace has been maintained by the Daughters of Hawaii since 1915. Open 9 a.m. to 4 p.m. Admission is $4. On Pali Highway, seven miles from Waikiki. Call 595-3167.

RABBIT ISLAND

Hare-raising experience

Sixty-seven-acre Manana is commonly called "Rabbit Island," either because of its shape or because it once was used for raising rabbits. Its smaller sister is 11-acre Kaohikaipu. Makapuu Point and Sea Life Park, 45 minutes from Waikiki, past Hanauma Bay.

RESTAURANT ROW

Elegant and ethnic eating

Restaurant Row occupies the ground floors of seven five-story office buildings overlooking Honolulu Harbor. Most of the space is allocated to eating—at elegant, ethnic, theme, indoor-outdoor and specialty restaurants. All this, plus fashion boutiques, coffee bars, snack carts, and a 1,250-car parking garage with free valet service. Open days and evenings, seven days a week. 500 Ala Moana Boulevard, about three miles from Waikiki.

ROYAL HAWAIIAN BAND

Established in 1836 by King Kamehameha III, this is the only royal band in the United States. It plays Hawaii's traditional melodies from monarchy days, classical music, and contemporary tunes. The band includes a string ensemble and a Big Band-era show band. Listen to a free concert every Friday at 12:15 p.m. on the grounds of Iolani Palace, King and Richards Streets, in downtown Honolulu. On the Waikiki Trolley route.

America's only royal band

You can also listen to the Royal Hawaiian Band at:
• 2 p.m. on Sunday at Kapiolani Park Bandstand.
• Noon on the first Wednesday of each month at Fort Street Mall.
• Noon on the second Wednesday at Ala Moana Shopping Center.
• Noon on the third Wednesday at Downtown Tamarind Park.

SACRED FALLS

Perpetual precipitation

Kaliuwaa, "sacred falls," has a sheer drop of 80 feet, in a 1,520-foot cascade. Hike approximately 30 minutes along Kaluanui Stream to the waterfall. No parking or entrance fees, but heed the warning signs in the parking area. About 75 minutes from Waikiki, past Kaaawa on your way to Laie and the Polynesian Cultural Center.

SAINT ANDREW'S CATHEDRAL

Nine decades to complete

Begun in 1867 under King Kamehameha IV (Liholiho) shortly after the tragic death of his four-year-old son, this stately high-church Episcopal cathedral of imported English sandstone took 91 years to finish. Stop and enjoy a moment of silence, and marvel at the beautiful stained glass. Open 6:30 a.m. to 6 p.m. Facing Queen Emma Square, at the intersection of Beretania and Alakea Streets in downtown Honolulu, it is about four miles, fifteen minutes, from Waikiki. The Waikiki Trolley and City Buses No. 1 and 2 stop at the State Capitol, one short block away. Call 524-2822.

SAINT LOUIS HEIGHTS

This mountain ridge flanking lush Manoa Valley offers a view of Diamond Head similar to but even closer than by Tantalus, its more famous neighbor. For a cool, relaxing afternoon of hiking or just admiring the view, seek out Waahila Ridge State Park at the top, off Ruth Place. Saint Louis Heights is the right wall of

Manoa Valley as you head toward the University of Hawaii. The City Bus (No. 14—St. Louis Heights) will take you there from the edge of Waikiki. Ask for directions at your hotel.

SANDY BEACH See Beaches.

SCHOFIELD BARRACKS

Home of the 25th Division

Named for Major General John M. Schofield, commander of the U.S. Army Division of the Pacific in the 1870s, and built in 1909, this 14,400-acre military installation is the home of the 25th Light Infantry "Tropic Lightning" Division, a rapid-strike force of nearly 11,000 men and women soldiers. Schofield Barracks is outside Wahiawa, at the end of H-2 about thirty miles from Waikiki.

SCUBA See Diving.

SEA LIFE PARK

Speeding cetaceans

This 62-acre ocean-theme park, with its exciting shows of trained sea lions, false killer whales, penguins, and porpoises, is an excellent place to spend the day. A giant 3,000-gallon reef tank has hundreds of different marine animals. Open 9:30 a.m. to 5 p.m. The hours are extended on Friday until 10 p.m. Admission for adults is $12.95; juniors, $8.50; children four to six, $4.50. At Makapuu Point on Kalanianaole Highway, thirty minutes from Waikiki. Call 923-1531 or 259-7933.

Open Friday nights

SNORKELING See Diving.

STREETS

Newcomers to Hawaii often find street names to be downright confusing. Familiarize yourself with the following major streets (especially the seven "K" streets), and your touring will be easier. These eleven streets cover 65 of Honolulu's major scenic spots!

Ala Moana Boulevard. This broad thoroughfare emerges Downtown from Nimitz Highway, heading toward Diamond Head past the Hawaii Maritime Museum, *Falls of Clyde*, Aloha Tower, Ala Moana Shopping Center and Ala Moana Beach Park, and ends by merging with Kalakaua Avenue in Waikiki. Just before it disappears, Kalia Road, where you will find the Hilton Hawaiian Village and the U.S. Army Museum, branches off to the right.

Downtown

Beretania Street. This busy one-way street begins in Moiliili and heads westward through Downtown along the way are the Honolulu Academy of Arts, Thomas Square, the State Capitol with the nearby Father Damien statue and the Eternal Flame, Washington Place, and Saint Andrew's Cathedral.

Kalakaua Avenue. This major street—one-way toward Diamond Head through Waikiki—extends from Punahou Street to the foot of Diamond Head Crater. The Royal Hawaiian Shopping Center, the International Market Place, Waikiki Beach, the Honolulu Zoo, the Waikiki Aquarium, Kapiolani Park, the Waikiki Shell and the Kodak Hula Show are landmarks along the way.

Kalanianaole Highway (Route 72, just "Kalani Hwy." to some) is a major highway from the Kahala end of Lunalilo Freeway (H-1), following the coast around the east end of Oahu through Hawaii Kai, past the Blowhole, around Makapuu Point, then northward along the Windward shore via Waimanalo, finally ending at the Castle Junction in Kailua. Major sights along this very scenic way include the Kahala residential area, Hanauma Bay and Koko Crater, the Blowhole and Sandy Beach, Makapuu Beach, Rabbit Island, and Sea Life Park.

Kapahulu Avenue runs inland along the Diamond Head edge of Waikiki. The Honolulu Zoo, Leonard's Bakery ("home of the perfect *malasada*"), the Ala Wai public golf course, and a gaggle of surfing, cycling and ethnic-food establishments, plus a few book shops, give the neighborhood special character.

Kapiolani Boulevard is another busy street that begins at the edge of Downtown and ends at the foot of Diamond Head. Along the way are many eating places, the Ala Moana Shopping Center, the city's Blaisdell Arena and Concert Hall, some handsome new office buildings, and prestigious Iolani School.

Kamehameha Highway (also known as "Kam Highway" or Route 83) teams up with Kalanianaole Highway to circle the island—around Makapuu, up the Windward side and along the North Shore, returning to Honolulu through Haleiwa, the Schofield Plateau and Pearl City. (Kahekili Highway is a shortcut from the Likelike Highway [Route 63] to Kahuluu.) Happily for economy-minded sightseers, the city bus system covers the entire circuit—all for 60 cents.

King Street is the eastbound counterpart of westbound Beretania Street between Downtown and Diamond Head. Major sights along the way are Maunakea Street with its street life, Tamarind Park, Iolani Palace and Barracks, the King Kamehameha statue, Kawaiahao Church, the Mission Houses Museum and the Blaisdell Concert Hall.

Kuhio Avenue is an important Waikiki artery, paralleling one-way Kalakaua Avenue just one block inland. It allows a second chance if you miss the turnoff to your hotel!

Lunalilo Freeway (H-1) is Honolulu's "spinal cord." It begins at Kahala, bisects Downtown, and passes Honolulu International Airport, Pearl Harbor, Aiea, Pearl City and Waipahu before finally merging with Farrington Highway on the Leeward coast. The Bishop Museum and U.S.S. *Arizona* Memorial are along the way.

The **Pali Highway** (Route 61) starts Downtown, goes over the Nuuanu Pali via the Pali Tunnel, and down to Kailua on the Windward side. Major attractions along the way are the National Cemetery of the Pacific (Punchbowl), Queen Emma's Summer Palace, Pali Lookout, Nuuanu Valley homes, Mount Olomana, Kailua, and Kailua Beach Park.

TANTALUS

A frustrating climb

Mt. Tantalus and Saint Louis Heights flank Manoa Valley. Rising 2,013 feet, Tantalus was named for the legendary Greek who, as punishment by the gods, was forced to stand up to his chin in water that would recede when he tried to drink. It apparently reflects the feelings of early climbers. Puu Ualakaa State Park on the south slope has one of the best views on Oahu.

To get to Tantalus from Waikiki, take Ala Wai Boulevard (one-way), making a right turn at the McCully bridge stoplight. Head toward the mountains approximately one mile, until McCully Street crosses Wilder Avenue at a stoplight. Head left on Wilder past Punahou School about a half mile to Makiki Street and turn right. Go straight up Makiki Street (ignoring Makiki Heights Drive) until you find yourself on Round Top Drive, which will lead you to Puu Ualakaa Park. Better yet: have someone show you the way! Puu Ualakaa Park is about twenty minutes from Waikiki—if you don't get lost.

TENNENT ART FOUNDATION GALLERY

Contains drawings, oils, and watercolors by the late Madge Tennent, gifted long-time resident of Hawaii. Guided tours, lectures, and library available. Open Tuesday through Saturday, 10 a.m. to noon; Sunday, 2 to 4 p.m.; and by appointment. No admission charge. At 203 Prospect Street, it is close to downtown Honolulu and about fifteen minutes from Waikiki. Call 531-1987.

TENNIS

Honolulu had 360 courts at last count. In 1990 the City & County controlled 175 of them at 46 facilities.

The closest public courts to Waikiki are in Kapiolani Park, opposite the Waikiki Aquarium. Recently refurbished, the four courts cater mostly to doubles play so the wait can be long.

Closer to Diamond Head crater, off Paki Avenue, is the more extensive Diamond Head Tennis Center with ten excellent courts, a clubhouse and shaded gallery, and a reservations sign-up sheet.

Ala Moana Park has eight courts, frequently crowded. Court courtesy allows 45 minutes for singles and 60 for doubles, including warm-up time.

If you cannot wait for a public court, try the luxury of private hotel or club facilities. While rates are lower for hotel guests, they still are pretty expensive.

TRANSPORTATION

TheBus

•The **Arizona Memorial Shuttle Bus** is available 6:30 a.m. to 10 p.m. The fare is $3 one way, $5 round trip. Call 926-4747 for schedule information.

•**Public Buses ("TheBus")**. Most of Oahu is accessible by the city bus system. Sixty-four lines provide economical transportation to such distant points as the Polynesian Cultural Center and other North Shore spots for the regular sixty-cent fare. You can do your own "circle-the-island" tour by catching the hourly No. 52 or No. 54 bus at Ala Moana Shopping Center, the main terminal and transfer point. The two services cover the same route in opposite directions.

Waikiki service begins as early as 5 a.m. and runs until midnight. Service hours and frequency may vary on other routes. Call 531-1611 for fare and schedule information.

•**Tour Buses**. If you want to leave the driving to someone else, commercial bus tours are available. For $20 to $56, you can visit the U.S.S. *Arizona* Memorial, see the highlights of Honolulu, Waimea Falls and the North Shore, go completely around the island, or combine several of the above. All tours have knowledgeable guides, include admission to most attractions, and provide hotel pickup. Your hotel tour desk has details and can make reservations.

•**Dole Cannery Square Bus.** Free pickup from 9 a.m. Tuesday, Wednesday, and Thursday at selected hotels for transport to Dole Cannery Square and back. Call 531-8855 for schedules.

•**Hilo Hattie Bus.** Free pickup from 9 a.m. Tuesday, Wednesday, and Thursday at selected hotels to see the Kodak Hula Show, Hilo Hattie Fashion Factory, the Dole Cannery, and Dole Pineapple Square. Call 537-2926.

•**Pineapple Transit.** Service every five minutes from 8:30 a.m. to 3:30 p.m. The fare is fifty cents. Many hotel pickups to Chinatown, Ward Warehouse, Ala Moana Shopping Center, Aloha Tower, Iolani Palace and, of course, the Dole Pineapple Cannery and Dole Cannery Square.

•**Taxis**. See General Information.

•**The Waikiki Trolley.** Service is from 9 a.m. to 4 p.m. The $15 all-day pass is good for a two-hour Honolulu Old Town Trolley Tour and a full day of riding aboard the 34-seat, open-air, motorized trolleys. Tours leave every 40 minutes from the Royal Hawaiian Shopping Center in central Waikiki, calling at the Hilton Hawaiian Village, Iolani Palace, Wo Fat (Chinatown), the State Capitol, King Kamehameha statue, the Mission Houses Museum, Aloha Tower, the Honolulu Academy of Arts, Hawaii Maritime Museum, Ward Centre, Fisherman's Wharf, and Restaurant Row. Call 526-0112.

TROPIC LIGHTNING MUSEUM

Depicts the history of Schofield Barracks and the U.S. Army's 25th Light Infantry Division. Open Tuesday through Saturday, 9 a.m. to 4 p.m., without charge. Located within Schofield Barracks, outside Wahiawa, about forty minutes from Waikiki. Call 655-0438.

UNIVERSITY OF HAWAII

Manoa campus

The University of Hawaii at Manoa is the heart of the State's nine-campus, 50,000-student university system. The 320-acre campus in Manoa Valley includes a law school, a medical school, two major libraries with more than two million volumes, an engineering facility, an extensive athletic plant, an Institute for Astronomy, and much more. Among its outstanding programs are marine biology, geophysics, linguistics, Oriental studies, travel industry management, and tropical agriculture. The East-West Center, although on the campus, is a separate, federally funded institution designed to promote understanding among the people of Asia, the Pacific, and the United States. The Office of University Relations, Bachman Annex 6,2444 Dole Street, Honolulu, Hawaii 96822 (or call 948-8856) can give you more information. The university is about twenty minutes from Waikiki.

The **University of Hawaii Art Gallery** contains traveling, student, and faculty exhibits. Open Monday through Friday, 10 a.m. to 4 p.m.; Sunday, 12 to 4 p.m. Closed holidays. No charge, but campus parking is involved. Located in the Art Building, University of Hawaii Manoa campus, three miles from Waikiki. Call 948-6888.

WAAHILA RIDGE STATE PARK

A little-known park, with a hiking trail and excellent views of Manoa Valley and Honolulu. Off Ruth Place at the top of Saint Louis Drive. Open from 7 a.m. to 6:45 p.m.

WAHIAWA

Vestiges of rural life remain in Wahiawa, a rapidly growing community that was home to about 44,000 in 1989. The U.S. Army Schofield Barracks and Wheeler Army Air Field are nearby, as are Wahiawa Botanical Garden and Kukaniloko, sacred birthing stones where royal Hawaiian women bore their children. Wahiawa is in the central Oahu plain, about thirty miles from Waikiki.

WAIANAE RANGE

The Hawaii of our dreams

The Waianae mountains, created 2,700,000-3,400,000 years ago, are the older and smaller of the two ranges that make up Oahu (the other is the Koolaus). Its Mount Kaala is the highest point on Oahu at 4,017 feet (1,224 meters).

WAIKIKI

Best-known beach

One-and-a-half-mile-long Waikiki ("spouting water"), measuring 0.7 square miles, has perhaps the best-known beach in the world. Originally mostly a swamp, its transformation began in 1922 when its springs were capped and the land behind the beach drained and filled. The present Ala Wai canal was dredged at the same time. By 1991, some 135 hotels and condominiums with 33,380 rooms—almost 45 percent of Hawaii's total 74,112 units—had made it the State's most densely developed community.

Most crowded community

WAIKIKI AQUARIUM

Newly renovated

Founded in 1904 and today part of the University of Hawaii, the Waikiki Aquarium is the third oldest in the United States. The aquarium's collections, exhibits, and research focus on the marine life of Hawaii and the South Pacific. Its tanks include more than 200 species, including sharks, giant clams, live coral, chambered nautilus, octopus, turkeyfish, and, of course, the *humuhumunukunukuapuaa*.

Among its unique displays are a living coral reef ecosystem (visitors are invited to touch the sea creatures); the Coastal Gardens, which contain rare and endangered Hawaiian coastal plants; and the highly acclaimed "Hawaiians and the Sea" display, which details the special relationship between the ancient Hawaiian culture and the sea. Open 9 a.m. to 5 p.m., closed Thanksgiving and Christmas. Admission charge. On Kalakaua Avenue, about ten minutes from central Waikiki, past the Honolulu Zoo. Call 923-9741.

WAIMANALO

Waimanalo is a small, relaxed, largely Hawaiian community of more than 9,000 off Kalanianaole Highway past Makapuu Point and Sea Life Park, on your way to Kailua. There's not much to see except scenery, but the atmosphere is friendly.

WAIMEA BAY See North Shore.

WAIMEA FALLS AND PARK

Waimea Falls is a forty-five foot waterfall on the North Shore, and is within the grounds of Waimea Falls Park.

The park covers 1,800 acres of trees, shrubs, and flowers from tropical and subtropical regions worldwide. It features exotic birds both in cages and out, Hawaiian dancers, cliff divers, botanical gardens, ancient Hawaiian living quarters and burial site, and tours. See daily *hula* dancing, cliff diving, and tours, along with special demonstrations and activities on selected holidays. Daily including Sundays and holidays, 10:00 a.m. to 5:30 p.m. Adults $14.95; Juniors six to twelve, $7.95; children under 5 free. At 59-864 Kamehameha Highway, Waimea, on the North Shore of Oahu, about forty miles or seventy minutes via Wahiawa from central Waikiki. Telephone 638-8511 or 923-8448 for more information.

WASHINGTON PLACE

'Little White House'

Completed in 1846 by Captain John Dominis, a New England ship captain and husband of Queen Lydia Kamakaena Liliuokalani, this stately mansion is now the official residence of Hawaii's governor. A two-story, 17-room porticoed building on three acres, it was named for George Washington and is sometimes called the "Little White House of the Pacific." Although it is not open to the public, it can easily be seen from South Beretania Street. About four miles from Waikiki, across the street from the State Capitol, where the Waikiki Trolley stops.

WO FAT

Venerable victuals

Around since 1882, this venerable restaurant is reputed to be Hawaii's oldest. It was and still is a landmark, reminiscent of Honolulu's original Chinatown. On Hotel Street, at the corner of Maunakea Street, less than twenty minutes from Waikiki. On the Waikiki Trolley and city bus routes. Call 533-6393 for reservations.

ZOO

See Honolulu Zoo.

HAWAII: A TIMELINE

750 A.D.

Polynesian settlers arrive in Hawaii, probably from the Marquesas Islands.

1100-1300

Frequent canoe voyages between Tahiti and Hawaii contribute to the growth of Hawaii's population.

1778

Captain James Cook and the crews of *Resolution* and *Discovery* sight Niihau and Kauai. They come ashore at Waimea, Kauai. Cook names the islands for his patron, the Earl of Sandwich. The following year, on a second visit to Hawaii, Cook with four seamen are killed at Kealakekua Bay on the island of Hawaii.

1795

Kamehameha I, with help from two English seamen and their guns, unites all the islands (except Kauai) under his rule, beginning the Kamehameha Dynasty.

1819

New England whaling ships arrive in Hawaii. Accession of Kamehameha II (Iolani Liholiho) and Queen Kaahumanu as joint rulers. Abolition of taboo system and idol worship.

1820

Henry Opukahaia, a young Hawaiian being educated in New England, dies in Cornwall, Connecticut, thereby inspiring the first mission of New England Congregationalists to Hawaii. Led by the Rev. Hiram Bingham, the party arrives on the Big Island on March 31 aboard the brig *Thaddeus*. A second group of American missionaries arrives in 1823.

1824

King Kamehameha II and his wife, Queen Kamamalu, die during a trip to England.

1825

Accession of Kamehameha IV. Queen Kaahumanu continuing as regent.

1846

Some 596 whaling vessels visit Hawaii. On one day in 1852, 131 whalers and 18 merchant ships are counted at Honolulu Harbor.

1848

A measles epidemic kills 10,000 people, mostly Hawaiians. Throughout the nineteenth century, outbreaks of venereal disease, measles, mumps, influenza, cholera, and smallpox take a heavy toll of the Hawaiians, who have little resistance to introduced diseases. From estimates of 300,000 to 500,000 at the time of Captain Cook, infant mortality, low fertility, and disease reduce the native population. By 1876, only 45,000 Hawaiians remained.

1861

The American Civil War boosts sugar prices. Hawaii's growing number of sugar plantations, advances in irrigation, refining, and shipping, as well as the arrival of Asian laborers, speed sugar's domination of the economic life of the Hawaiian Kingdom.

1863

The accession of Kamehameha V.

1866

The first leprosy patients are put ashore at Kalawao Peninsula (Kalaupapa) on Molokai, to be kept in isolation. By 1873 the colony has 800 patients. In that year, Father Damien, a Belgian priest, arrives to minister to the patients. He dies there of leprosy in 1889.

1866

The first leprosy patients are put ashore at Kalawao Peninsula (Kalaupapa) on Molokai, to be kept in isolation. By 1873 the colony has 800 patients. In that year, Father Damien, a Belgian priest, arrives to minister to the patients. He dies there of leprosy in 1889.

1873

William C. Lunalilo elected King—the last of the Kamehameha dynasty.

1874

The election of David Kalakaua to the Hawaiian throne results in a riot by disappointed followers of Dowager Queen Emma.

1886

Commercial pineapple production begins with small plantations at Waipahu and Manoa in Honolulu, and a cannery. The venture fails. Successful pineapple cultivation will begin in 1901.

The first great wave of Japanese arrives to work on sugar plantations. By 1896 Japanese will account for one-fourth of the Islands' population.

1893

Queen Liliuokalani is deposed, marking the end of The Hawaiian monarchy. A provisional government is set up under Sanford B. Dole. The Republic of Hawaii lasts until July 7, 1898, when President McKinley signs a joint congressional resolution annexing Hawaii to the United States as a territory. The population at the time of annexation will be roughly 110,000.

1901

The first Hawaiian songs ("Aloha Oe" and "Pua i Kaoakalani") are recorded by Columbia Records. Electric streetcars replace Honolulu's horse-drawn trolleys. Construction begins on Honolulu's first high-rise, the six-story Moana Hotel at Waikiki Beach. The gracious wooden landmark, home of the long-running "Hawaii Calls" radio program, will be fully restored 90 years later.

1908

The construction of a U.S. naval base at Pearl Harbor is authorized.

1927

A U.S. Army C-23 Wright trimotor plane makes the first nonstop flight from the mainland U.S. to Hawaii. The first commercial passenger flight to the mainland will occur in 1935.

1940

The fifth federal census reveals an island population of 423,330. A plebiscite during the general election of that year shows 2-to-1 support for statehood.

1941-1944

Japanese aircraft and submarines attack Pearl Harbor and other military installations on December 7, killing 2,323 servicemen and 60 civilians, and the U.S. declares war on Japan. Three weeks after the attack, Japanese submarines shell the ports of Hilo, Nawiliwili, and Kahului. Hawaii is placed under marshal law amid fears of a Japanese invasion. In June 1942, the Japanese fleet is defeated in the Battle of Midway, a decisive turning point in the war in the Pacific. The buildup of military forces in Hawaii during World War II reaches 400,000 service men and women.

1946

Hawaii's most destructive tsunami strikes the northern shores of all islands, most seriously at Hilo on the Big Island, killing 175 people and causing $25,000,000 damage. The wave at Hilo is measured at 55 feet above sea level.

1954

The Democratic Party, organized by labor leaders and representatives of Hawaii's large Japanese middle class, sweeps the territorial elections, ending an era of Republican dominance.

1959

President Eisenhower signs the Statehood Enabling Act on March 18. Statehood becomes official June 27 when island residents vote 17-to-1 for statehood.

Pan American and Qantas Airlines begin jet service to Hawaii, ushering in Hawaii's tourism boom years.

1966

Live television from the mainland is inaugurated with a football game via satellite. Visitors total one million; by 1989 the figure will be six million.

In the Vietnam War, Honolulu becomes an "R & R" (rest and recreation) center for U.S. troops.

1970

New jumbo passenger jets create jumbo hotels: The 1,800-room Sheraton Waikiki is completed at Waikiki Beach. The federal census shows a population of 770,000.

1976

The Hawaiian Renaissance: Hawaiian activists rally to stop Navy bombing of Kahoolawe Island. The sailing canoe *Hokulea* voyages to Tahiti and back without modern navigational tools, relying instead on arts handed down from the ancient Polynesians. The 1970s are marked by increased native Hawaiian protests against what they consider to be the misuse of their land, and there is a resurgent interest in pre-contact Hawaiian arts, crafts, and dance forms. The *hula* is reinvigorated, stressing authentic styles and a renewed respect for the spiritual and social importance of the dance.

1982

Kilauea volcano begins a sustained eruption, adding hundreds of acres of new land to the Big Island and destroying subdivisions, archaeological sites, and a visitor's center at Hawaii Volcanoes National Park. The slow-moving lava flow becomes a popular continuing tourist attraction.

Hurricane Iwa rips the islands with 117-mph winds. Hardest hit is the island of Kauai, where the tourist industry suffers severe damage.

1986

Hawaii elects its first Hawaiian governor, Democrat John Waihee, and its first Filipino lieutenant governor, Democrat Ben Cayetano. Hawaii's population reaches 1,000,000.

1989

Hawaii celebrates 30 years of statehood.

1992

Hurricane Iniki devastates the island of Kauai on September 11.

GLOSSARY OF HAWAIIAN WORDS

The Hawaiian language is much like the islands themselves—poetic, mellifluous, easy on the senses. It is, in fact, one of the world's most beautiful languages.

To the old Hawaiians, language was much more than just a way to say "pass the *poi*." It was also the primary means of passing along the culture. Much of what we know of early Hawaiiana has come from chants, legends and other forms of oral history handed down from generation to generation.

Today, after two centuries of western influence in the islands, Hawaiian is generally heard only in music, except for certain words which have become permanent staples. A notable exception occurs on the privately owned island of Niihau, where Hawaiian is the language of choice for the community of 200 full-blooded Hawaiians. And, fortunately, recent years have seen a great resurgence of interest in Hawaiian language studies at the University of Hawaii and in secondary schools throughout the State.

At first glance, Hawaiian words may seem formidable. The State fish, after all, is the *humuhumunukunukuapuaa*, and anyone driving from Waikiki to Hanauma Bay must contend with Kalanianaole Highway. But the fact is that pronunciation is guided by an easy-to-learn, unchanging set of rules. The five vowels, for instance, are always pronounced like so: "a" as in *father*, "e" as in *they*, "i' as in *bikini*, "o" as in *no*, and "u" as in *rule*.

In today's common usage, the language has only eight consonants, although the old Hawaiians actually used more. When the first Christian missionaries encountered Hawaiian early in the nineteenth century, they set about putting this previously oral language into written form, all the better to translate the Bible and convert these far-flung islands, they reasoned. In the interests of facility, the well-meaning evangelists cut a few corners, leaving behind "r" (which then was interchangeable with "l"), the "t," the "b," and probably a few others. This is one of the main reasons that spelling and pronunciation are the subjects of such lively discussion among today's Hawaiian-language scholars.

More and more these days you will see the glottal stop, the reverse apostrophe that appears between vowels in certain words. The glottal stop signals a subtle catch in the voice between two vowels, just as in the English interjection, "oh-oh." It can make a big difference. *Pau* (pronounced "pow") means "finished." *Pa'u* ("pa-oo") is a ceremonial riding skirt.

Throughout your island travels you will encounter many Hawaiian words which have become integral parts of the vernacular. You may have trouble picking a restroom unless you know the difference between a *kane (*man*)* and a *wahine (*woman*)*. And despite what many visitors think when they see a public garbage can for the first time, *mahalo* means "thank you," not "trash."

From Memories of Hawaii, *reprinted courtesy of Pleasant Travel Service.*

Ahu ula- Feather cape.
Aina- Land.
Akaku- Vision; reflection.
Akamai (AH-ka-MEYE)-
Smart; clever; quick.
Ala- Fragrant; per
fumed; also road, path.
Alii (a-LEE-i)- Hawaiian
royalty.
Aloha (a-LOH-ha)-
Hello; goodbye; love;
affection; welcome.
Anuenue- Rainbow.
Apana- Piece; land
division.
Aumakua- Family or
personal god.
Auwai- Ditch.
Auwana- To wander.
Auwe (ow-WAY)- An
exclamation: oh! alas!
dear me!
Ewa (EH-va)- Toward
Leeward Oahu;
unstable;wandering.
Halau- Hula school;
canoe house.
Hale- House; building.
Hana- Bay; valley.
Hanai- Adopted.
Haole (HOW-le)-
Foreigner; white
person.
Hapa (HAH-pa)-Half, a
person of mixed race
may be referred to as
hapa-haole, "half white."
Hapai- Pregnant.
Heiau (HEH-i-YOW)-
Hawaiian temple.
Hele mai (HEH-le
MEYE)- Come!
Hoku- Star.
Holoholo- To walk.
Holoku- Long gown.
Hoolaulea- Celebration.
Huhu (HOO-HOO)-
Angry.
Hui- Club; association.

Hukilau- Net fishing.

Hula- A dance.

Ili ili- Pebble(s).
Imu (EE-moo)- Under
ground oven where pig
and other food is cooked
for a luau.
Io- Hawk.
Ipo- Sweetheart.

Ipu- Gourd.

Ipu hokiokio- Gourd
whistle.
Kahiko- Old; ancient.

*Kahuna (ka-HOO-na)-
Hawaiian priest; a sorcerer.*

Kai- Sea; sea water.
Kalaau- Stick dance.
Kamaaina (kah-ma-
EYE-nah)- Native-born
or longtime resident.

Kanaka (ka-NAH-ka)-
Man; commoner.
Kane (KAH-ne)- Male,
man.
Kapa- Bark cloth (tapa).
Kapu (KAH-pu)-
Forbidden; taboo.

Keiki (KAY-ki)- Baby; child.

Kii- Picture; photograph.
Kilu- Gourd; coconut
shell.
Koa- *Acacia koa*,
endemic forest tree; a
warrior.
Kokua (ko-KOO-wa)-
Help.
Kona (KOH-na)-
Leeward shore.
Koolau- Windward shore.
Kuhina- Minister;
premier.
Kumu- Teacher.

*Kupuna- Grandparent;
ancestor.*

Lanai (la-NEYE)-
Outdoor porch; veranda.

*Lauhala- Pandanus leaf
used in plaiting.*

Lei (LAY)- Flower
wreath; necklace.
Limu- Seaweed.
Lua- Outhouse; toilet.

Luau (LOO-OW)- Ha-waiian feast; party.

Luna- Boss.
Mahalo (ma-HAH-lo)-
Thank you
Mahalo nui loa (NOO-i
LOH-a)- Thank you very
much.
Mahele- Portion; division.
Mahimahi- Dolphin fish.
Mahiole- Feather helmet.
Makahiki- Ancient
Hawaiian fall festival.
Makai (ma-KEYE)-
Toward the ocean.
Makani- Wind; breeze.
Malihini (ma-li-HEE-ni)-
Newcomer to the islands.

Malo- Loincloth.

Mana- Supernatural or
divine power.
Mano- Shark.
Manu- Bird.
Mauka (MOW-ka)-
Toward the mountains.
Mauna- Mountain;
mountainous.

Mele- Song: peom.
Mehehune- Legendary
"small people."
Moana- Ocean.

Muumuu- Loose gown.

Nane- Riddle; puzzle;
parable.
Nei- Here; this place.
Nui- Large; great;
important.

Ohana- Family.

Ohe hanoihu- Nose flute.
Okole- Buttocks.
Ono (OH no)- Delicious.
Opu- Stomach.
Pahu- Drum.
Palaka- Indifferent; in-active. Also check
ered cloth.
Pali- Cliff; precipice.

*Paniolo (PAH-ni-OH-lo)-
Hawaiian cowboy.*

Papa hehi- Treadle
board.
Pau (POW)- Finished; end.
Pele- Lava flow; the
volcano goddess.

Pikake- Jasmine.
Piko- Navel; umbilical
cord.
Pili- To cling. Also
grass for house thatch.
Pilikia (PEE-li-KEE-ya)-
Trouble.
Pohaku- Rock; stone.

*Poi (POY)- Pounded
taro root.*

Pua- Flower.
Pueo- Owl.
Puili- Bamboo rattle.
Puka (POO-ka)- Hole;
gate; door.
Punee- Couch.
Pupu (POO-pu)-
Appetizer; shellfish.
Pupule- Insane.
Tutu- Grandmother; aunt.
Ua- Rain.

Ukulele- String instrument.

Uli uli- Gourd rattle
with feather.
Wahine (wa-HEE-ne)-
Female; woman.
Wene- Glow.
Wikiwiki (WEE-ki
WEE-ki)- Quickly;
speedy; hurry.

Heliconia

FLORA

Even the most jaded home gardener never fails to react with amazement to Hawaii's bewildering variety of trees, shrubs and flowers. Some plants are endemic, that is, found naturally nowhere else, having evolved into special Hawaiian forms from seeds that floated ashore or were carried by birds. Many others were brought here by early Polynesians in their voyages from the South Pacific. And still others arrived as deliberate imports in the two centuries of western contact. All today are part of the Islands' flora.

A few of the less familiar trees and flowers you will see as you move about the Islands are:

AFRICAN TULIP TREE
(Spathodea companulata)

A native of tropical Africa, this tall tree is distinctive with its brilliant red-orange displays. Large five-petaled flowers, with edges trimmed in yellow, surround clusters of crescentic buds.

ANTHURIUM
(Anthurium andraeanum)

This colorful, popular and long-lasting member of the arum family is sometimes called the flamingo flower. A central fingerlike white-to-yellow spike is surrounded by a heart-shape collar (bract) that ranges from white to brilliant red. Its tiny flowers are packed tightly on the central spike and often go unnoticed. Anthuriums are popular as gifts or for mailing home.

BANYAN *(Ficus spp.)*

An evergreen member of the Ficus family from India, banyans are easily identified by its aerial roots that hang to the ground and eventually take root. These in turn become additional weight-bearing trunks that allow the tree to spread. Excellent examples of the a banyan is are behind Iolani Palace in downtown Honolulu, at nearby Thomas Square, and in the center of Lahaina on Maui.

BIRD OF PARADISE
(Strelitzia reginae)

A relative of the banana, this distinctive flower can be seen in gardens everywhere. With its large paddle-shaped leaves and long-neck flowers resembling a bird's head and crest, the orange variety is easily recognizable. The flower sheath that resembles the bird's beak holds as many as six flowers.

BOUGAINVILLEA *(Bouganvillea spp.)*

A native of Brazil, this hardy member of the four-o'clock family named for Louis de Bougainville (an eighteenth century French navigator) is found throughout the Islands. The vivid leaf colors—red, crimson, orange, white, deep lavender, pink—are boldly splashed in thick sprays. These modified (leaves) surround the tiny flowers. Bougainvillea is a pleasure to see, but a challenge for gardeners to prune. Watch out for the thorns!

BREADFRUIT
(Artocarpus communis)

This handsome tree, which the Hawaiians call *ulu,* belongs to the mulberry family and can grow to sixty feet. It is an ancient Polynesian introduction to the Islands. The fruit weighs up to ten pounds and has a sweet mealy pulp, somewhat like a sweet potato. The light wood from its trunk was used in the old days to make drums, surfboards, canoes, and houses.

BROMELIAD

Almost all of these relatives of the pineapple—named for Olaf Bromel, a Swedish botanist—are native to South America and the Caribbean. A large and ubiquitous family, its approximately 1,400 species are found in deserts, rain forests, and semi-arid savannahs. Most are epiphytes (air plants) thriving on rain, air, and the organic debris from plants around them. A limited number grow as other plants do, rooted in the ground. The pineapple is the most famous and commercially important member of the bromeliad family.

COCONUT *(Cocos nucifera)*

Known as *niu* to the Hawaiians (*Cocos nucifera* to the botanists), the coconut tree's slender, graceful trunk and rustling fronds are an icon for the tropics worldwide. The Hawaiians took full advantage of the coconut palm. The trunk was used to make drums, food containers, small canoes, and houses, and the leaves went into baskets, fans, balls, and brooms, not to mention thatch for houses. The fibrous husk that protects the actual nut was twisted and braided into rope. The shell was fashioned into spoons, bowls, and small knee drums. The coconut is undoubtedly best known, however, for its meat, used commonly in cooking as a garnish, as a flavoring, and to make a delicious Hawaiian pudding, *haupia*.

Believe it or not, the U.S. Postal Service will accept a coconut for mailing. Write the address directly on the husk and take it to the post office.

COFFEE *(Coffea arabica)*

The only coffee grown commercially in the United States is from Hawaii's Kona district on the Big Island (although experimental planting has started on Maui and Kauai). Originally from Arabia and Ethiopia, it was introduced in 1813 by Don Francisco Marin, a business adviser to King Kamehameha the Great. While on the Big Island, visit a plantation near the village of Captain Cook, south of Kona.

CROTON *(Codiaeum variegatum)*

One of the novelties of the tropics is the croton shrub. Its shiny, multicolored leaves, in vivid splotchy combinations of green, yellow, and fuchsia, are favorites for hedges or ornamentals. Horticulturalists have created hundreds of varieties whose leaf shapes include broad, narrow, and curly.

GINGER FLOWER

All members of the ginger family have blade-shaped leaves and fibrous, reedlike stalks, reminding us that they are closely related to the banana. Ever-blooming red ginger (*Alpinia purpurata*) carries its foot-high head of red bracts upright like a feather duster, while shell ginger (*A. zerumbet*) has grapelike clusters of inch-long white buds resembling porcelain shells. Torch ginger (*Etlingera elatior*), a red-or pink-flowered imitation of a torch, is probably the most distinctive. Delicate yellow and white ginger blossoms are often strung into wonderfully scented leis. The flowers wilt within a day, but their delightful fragrance lingers for weeks.

GUAVA *(Psidium guajava)*

This member of the berry family was brought to Hawaii from Central America by the indefatigable Don Francisco Marin. A glass of ice-cold guava juice will tell you why it is an all-time favorite. They grow abundantly along rural roadsides and in pastures.

187

HELICONIA

Also related to bananas, heliconias have large paddle-shaped leaves and fibrous reedlike stalks. The most distinctive species includes the many varieties of large lobster claws (*Heliconia bihai*), with their five-inch crimson-red bracts that resemble boiled lobster claws. Other heliconias are pink, green, and deep orange yellow.

HIBISCUS *(Hibiscus spp.)*

An estimated 5,000 varieties, including several native species, bloom in Hawaii today. A smallish native red species was designated the official flower of the Territory of Hawaii back in 1923 and continued to be recognized after statehood in 1959. The flower lasts for one day only, picked or not, and with or without water.

ILIMA *(Sida fallax)*

This low-growing relative of the hibiscus produces pale yellow-to-orange blossoms that, in the old days, only Hawaiian chiefs were allowed to wear. Today *ilima* is a popular lei flower. The island of Oahu (Honolulu) has designated *ilima* as its official flower.

JADE VINE
(Strongylodon macrobotrys)

Elegant sprays of blue and jade-green flowers identify this vine, a member of the pea family. Its two-inch flowers, resembling tiger claws, make a long-lasting lei. A red jade vine also grows in Hawaii.

KOA *(Acacia koa)*

With its curved leaves resembling eucalyptus, the *koa* is Hawaii's tallest and probably finest native tree. Its reddish brown wood was carved into bowls and platters, and entire trunks were hollowed out for ocean-going canoes. Once plentiful, the

MACADAMIA NUT TREE
(Macadamia ternifolia)

Native to Australia and named for botanist John MacAdam, Hawaii's first macadamia trees were planted by W.H. Purvis
in 1881, on his farm at Honokaa on the
Big Island.The shell is hard to break
without crushing the meat, and exploi-
tation had to wait until 1939 when a
mechanical cracker was invented. Try
macadamia nuts in candies and pies,
slivered as a garnish, or just eat them
right out of the tin.

MANGO *(Mangifera indica)*

Originally from India, the common mango
was brought to Hawaii by Don Francisco
Marin, who also gave us coffee and the
guava. The trees grow to seventy feet and
are easily identified during the growing
season by their maroon young leaves. The
fruit is wonderfully tasty. Beware, however, if you are allergic to poison oak, ivy
or sumac. The mango skin and milky sap
contain similar allergens.

BEACH NAUPAKA
(Scaevola sericea)

This hardy shrub is common along
Hawaii's shores just above the high-tide
line where its bright-green leaves seem
to drink up the salt air. Native to the
Pacific islands, the small white *naupaka*
flowers are curiously shaped, as if half
the blossom had been torn away. Hawaiians tell of two mortal lovers separated
by a jealous god. When the lovers are
reunited, so the legend goes, the *naupaka*
flower will again be whole.

great *koa* groves of the Big Island are
disappearing in the wake of increased demand for the elegant wood as paneling,
doors, flooring, and trim, as well as for
ceremonial bowls and trophies.

KUKUI *(Aleurites moluccana)*

The candlenut tree arrived in Hawaii with
the early Polynesians, who used its oil-
rich kernels in torches. Kernels were also
roasted and eaten as a laxative. The hard
black-brown nuts, polished until they
gleam like ebony, make a striking traditional lei. The tall *kukui* tree, distin-
guished by its pale gray-green canopy,
can be spotted in groves along stream
beds in the mountains. It is Hawaii's
State tree.

OHIA *(Metrosideros collina)*

A true native of Hawaii, this ubiqitous
native tree prefers moist environments
and can be found from sea level to all
but the highest mountains. Popular in
songs and stories, the spiky, pompom-
shaped red blossom (*ohia lehua*) is be-
lieved to be sacred to Pele, the Hawaiian
goddess of volcanoes. Its very hard, dark-
red wood was used for mallets, spears
and religious statues.

ORCHID

The Big Island, often called the Orchid Isle, is a leading exporter of the flowers which are grown under massive gauze tents in the forest above Hilo. Driving through wetter parts of the island you will occasionally see small, pale purple-and-white orchids growing wild. Orchids are everywhere in Hawaii—strung in the lei that greets you as you step off your plane, tucked behind the ear of your hostess, floating in your drink at a *luau*, perhaps resting on your pillow when you turn in for the night. Of some 25,000 orchid species known worldwide, *Cattleyas*, *Vanda*, and *Dendrobiums* are the most common here.

PANDANUS
(Pandanus odoratissimus)

The pandanus tree (*hala*) arrived in Hawaii early with the Polynesians. The fibrous shiny leaves of this palmlike tree, when dried and properly prepared, are woven into *lauhala* mats, hats, baskets, and handbags. Fine hats woven from the rare red *lauhala* make exceptional—and expensive—gifts. On female trees, the fruit grows in tight clusters resembling pineapples. The Hawaiians used the dried fruit for paint brushes and the tips of its aerial roots in medicines.

PAPAYA *(Carica papaya)*

This delectable fruit (*mikana, milikana,* or *hei* to Hawaiians) also goes by the name *pawpaw*. It grows on palm-like trunks that vary in height from five to twenty-five feet, depending on their age, location, and variety. Its milky sap contains papain, an enzyme used in meat tenderizers. To really appreciate this wonderful fruit, try a chilled half sprinkled with lime juice for breakfast.

PASSION FRUIT *(Passiflora edulis)*

Locally called *lilikoi*, after the Maui district to which the purple variety is said to have been introduced from Brazil, the leathery, egg-sized passion fruit is filled with tiny seeds that yield a delicious tart juice. If you have a sweet tooth, try a piece of passion-fruit cake or a tall glass of cold passion-fruit juice.

PIKAKE *(Jasminum sambac)*

A member of the olive family and a true jasmine, this elegantly scented flower is very short-lived. A lei of *pikake* (supposedly the Hawaiian pronunciation of "peacock") is appropriate for a wedding or a prom. The Chinese use jasmine to scent tea.

PLUMERIA *(Plumeria spp.)*

Named for the French botanist Plumier and known in British parlance as "*frangipani*," these fragrant five-petalled flowers are among the most popular lei flowers. Native to tropical America, this member of the periwinkle family can be seen everywhere in the Islands. New trees are planted from branch cuttings. Be careful of its milky sap. Skin contact can cause an itchy rash.

SHOWER TREE *(Cassia spp.)*

The spectacular pink-and-white, coral, golden and rainbow shower trees are all members of the legume family. Big blossom clusters, blooming from late spring through the summer, overwhelm the young leaves with cascades of vivid color. Shower trees grow along city streets and suburban roads throughout Hawaii. "Shower-tree season" offers one of the State's most spectacular floral displays.

TARO *(Colocasia esculenta)*

This starchy, tuberous, unprepossessing root—a staple food of ancient Hawaiians—was brought here by the original Polynesian settlers. Its roots are still used to make *poi*, that sticky blob next to the *kalua* pork on your *luau* plate. Its nutritious spinach-like leaves are cooked as greens and made into medicine. The State produces more than 6 million pounds of *taro* a year, with a recent market value of $1,900,000.

TI *(Cordyline terminalis)*

Placed close to a home, *ti* is thought to protect a family from evil spirits. You will see it guarding rural (and many urban) homes. Growing abundantly in island lowlands, it is an important traditional garden plant. Its strong, flexible paddle-shaped leaves had many uses for the early Hawaiians, who brought it from southern Polynesia. Today, *ti* leaves are used in simple plaited lei, *hula* skirts, placemats, as an all-purpose greenery on parade floats, banquet tables and room separators, and to wrap food to be cooked in an underground oven. Until only a few decades ago, alcoholic *okolehao* was brewed from its fermented roots.

Aloha Stadium– home of the 1992 WAC champion
University of Hawaii Rainbow football team

ATTENDANCE AT MAJOR CULTURAL ATTRACTIONS

OAHU

National Memorial Cemetery (1991)	5,522,948
U.S.S. *Arizona* Memorial	1,635,591
Polynesian Cultural Center	838,000
Honolulu Zoo	704,424
Sea Life Park	638,973
Waimea Falls Park	458,131
Bernice Pauahi Bishop Museum	509,627
Dole Cannery Square	562,000
Waikiki Aquarium	317,962
Paradise Cove Luau Park (1990)	250,354
U.S.S. *Bowfin* WWII Submarine Exhibit	205,525
Mormon Temple Grounds	159,180
Honolulu Academy of Arts	259,278
U.S. Army Museum, Ft. DeRussy	125,576
Iolani Palace State Monument	72,000
Hoomaluhia Park	63,300
Foster Botanic Garden	69,226
University of Hawaii Art Gallery	50,000
Senator Fong's Plantation and Gardens	95,450
Contemporary Art Museum	41,050
Mission Houses Museum	30,536
Queen Emma Summer Palace	15,155
Wahiawa Botanical Garden	22,501
Waipahu Cultural Garden Park	34,150
Harold Lyon Arboretum	28,450
Damien Museum and Archives	13,221
Moanalua Gardens Foundation (1990)	21,600
Puu o Mahuka Heiau State Monument	4,000
Hawaii Maritime Center	74,487

HAWAII

Jagger Museum (1991)	1,150,000
Kilauea Visitor Center (1991)	375,000
Volcano Art Center	72,500
Panaewa Rainforest Zoo	84,234
Lapakahi State Historical Park	108,000
Kealakekua Bay State Historical Park	191,000
Hawaii Tropic Botanical Gardens	53,500
Parker Ranch Visitor Center	17,725
Hulihee Palace	24,669
Lyman House Memorial Museum	19,007
Greenwell Store Museum	5,000

MAUI

Maui Tropical Plantation	369,887
Whalers Village Museum	233,581
Maui Zoological and Botanical Gardens	46,000
Brig *Carthaginian II* (1990)	48,400
(Lahaina Restoration Foundation)	
Baldwin Missionary Home Museum (1990)	47,667
(Lahaina Restoration Foundation)	
Halekii-Pihana Heiaus State Monument	7,000
Wo Hing Temple (1990)	43,400
(Lahaina Restoration Foundation)	
Alexander & Baldwin Sugar Museum	29,679
Kalaupapa Lighthouse Exhibit (1990)	12,600
(Lahaina Restoration Foundation)	
Kula Gardens	19,790
Maui Historical Society Museum (1990)	14,207
Hale Paahao (Old Lahaina Prison) (1990)	30,770
(Lahaina Restoration Foundation)	
Hale Wai Wai o Hana (Hana Cultural Center)	8,191
Hale Pai (1990)	4,800
(Lahaina Restoration Foundation)	

KAUAI

Russian Fort Elizabeth State Historical Park	310,000
Kokee Natural History Museum	68,582
Kauai Museum	29,665
National Tropical Botanical Garden	30,420
Grove Farm Homestead	2,959
Waioli Mission House	1,595
Haraguchi Rice Mill Museum (1990)	1,265

MOLOKAI

Kalaupapa Settlement	8,982
Molokai Ranch Wildlife Park	3,894
R. W. Meyer Sugar Mill	2,646

Source:
The State of Hawaii Data Book, 1992

p. 2 - Reef Triggerfish (Baker-Van Dyke Collection); p. 9 - Currency (Randy Mita); p. 10 - Closet City (Randy Mita); p. 13 - Heliconia (Randy Mita); p. 15 - Golf (Mauna Lani Bay Hotel); p. 23 - Mission House (Randy Mita); p. 24 - Monarchy Photos (Baker-Van Dyke Collection); p. 27 - The Brothers Cazimero (Norman Shapiro); p. 37 - Shells (Waikiki Aquarium); p. 41 - Ukulele (Randy Mita); p. 43 - Zori (Randy Mita); p. 80 - Iniki (Bruce Asato/Honolulu Advertiser); p. 82 - Haena Point (Scott Rutherford); p. 117 - Kipahulu (Scott Rutherford); p. 123 - Kalaupapa Village (Hawaii State Archives); p. 125 - Saint Philomena Church (Hawaii State Archives); p. 127 - Niihau Shell (A. Kay Kepler); p. 137 - Dole Cannery (John Demello); p. 142 - Rainfall (Scott Rutherford); p. 144 - Aloha Tower (Scott Rutherford); p. 147 - Natural Science Center (Geraldine Garretson); p. 149 - The Contemporary Museum (Contemporary Museum); p. 153 - Japanese Garden (Randy Mita); p. 155 - Haiku Garden (Randy Mita); p. 160 - Sugar Mill (Randy Mita); p. 166 - Body Sailing (Randy Mita); p. 168 - Summer Palace (Randy Mita); p. 170 - St. Andrew's (Randy Mita); p. 171 - Open Friday Nights (Martin and Assoc.); p. 175 - UH (Randy Mita); p. 185 - Breadfruit (Randy Mita); p. 186 - Coconut (Randy Mita); p. 187- Ilima (Randy Mita); p. 187 - Guava (Randy Mita); p. 189 - Mango (Randy Mita); p. 189 - Orchid (Randy Mita); pp. 178-180 - Hawaii Timeline (Hawaii State Archives); p. 180 - First Hawaiian Governor (Honolulu Advertiser/ Ken Sakamoto).